ADVENTUROUS
IN
DEVON

Michael Bennie

COUNTRYSIDE BOOKS
NEWBURY BERKSHIRE

First published 2003

COUNTRYSIDE BOOKS
3 Catherine Road
Newbury, Berkshire

To view our complete range of books,
please visit us at
www.countrysidebooks.co.uk

ISBN 1 85306 786 5

Cover illustration by Paul Vale
Maps and photographs by the author
Designed by Peter Davies, Nautilus Design

Typeset by Techniset Typesetters, Newton-le-Willows
Produced through MRM Associates Ltd., Reading
Printed by J. W. Arrowsmith Ltd., Bristol

Contents

INTRODUCTION 6

Walk

1 The Wreckers' Coast: Berrynarbor to Ilfracombe (7 miles) *The Olde Globe* 8

2 Doone Country: North-western Exmoor (12 miles) *The Rockford Inn* 14

3 Strip Farming, Sea Shells and Sand Dunes: Braunton Burrows to Croyde ($10\frac{1}{2}$ miles) *The Thatch* 21

4 Shipwrecks and Saints: Devon's West Coast ($9\frac{1}{4}$ miles) *The Hartland Quay Hotel* 27

5 Wide Skies and Open Spaces: Exmoor's Southern Fringe (12 miles) *The London Inn* 33

6 In the Footsteps of the Otter: The Tarka Trail at Torrington ($10\frac{1}{2}$ miles) *The Clinton Arms* 39

7 The Engineers and the Eccentric: The Grand Western Canal and the Exe Valley Way ($10\frac{1}{2}$ miles) *The Butterleigh Inn* 45

8 Mists, Myths and Mysteries: Belstone Common and Skaigh Wood ($7\frac{1}{2}$ miles) *The Oxenham Arms* 51

9 Woods and Water: The Teign Gorge ($11\frac{1}{2}$ miles) *The Fingle Bridge Inn* 57

10 Faithless Wives and Fickle Maidens: The South and North Teign Rivers ($11\frac{3}{4}$ miles) *The Northmore Arms* 63

11 East Devon's Pebblebed Heath: Woodbury and East Budleigh Commons ($7\frac{1}{4}$ miles) *The Sir Walter Raleigh* 70

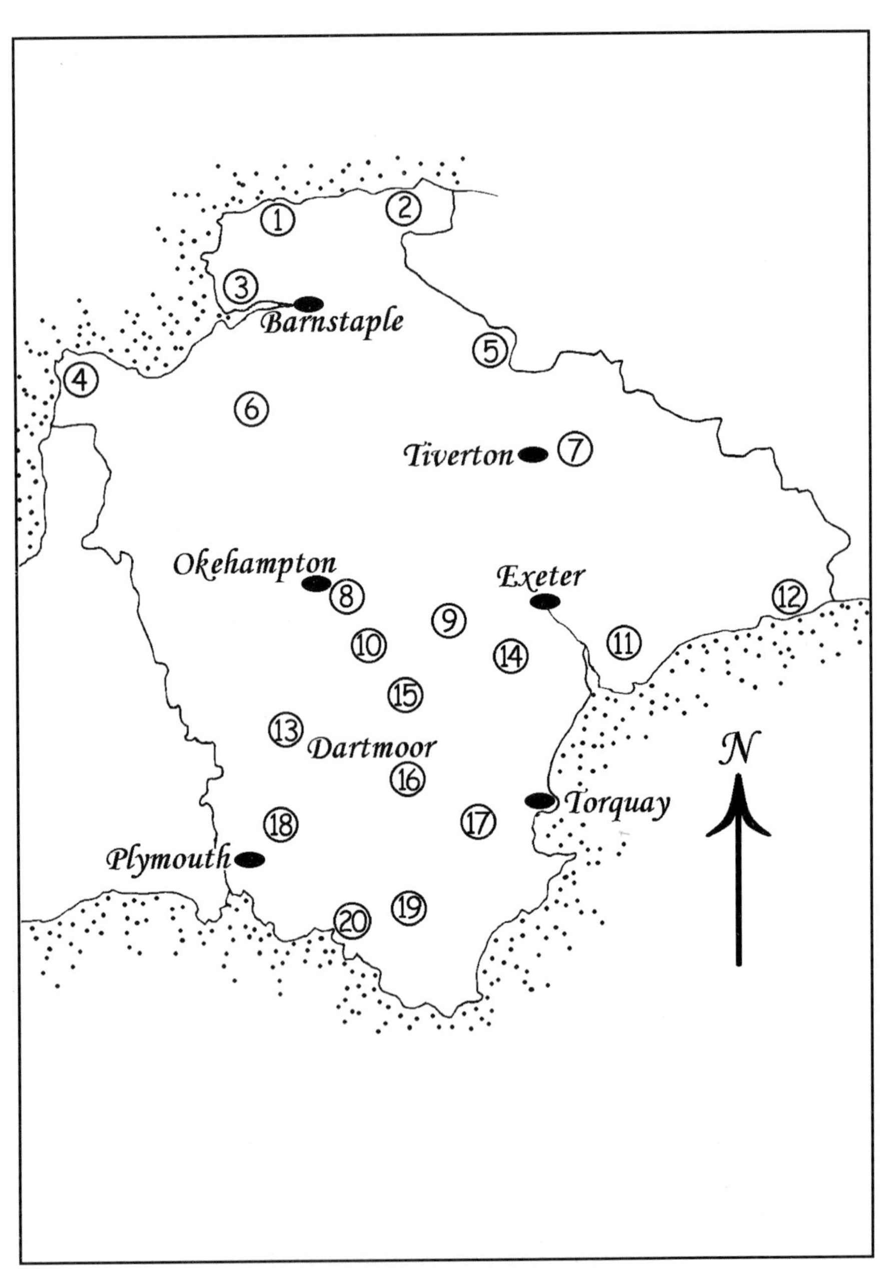

AREA MAP SHOWING THE LOCATION OF THE WALKS

12 The Undercliff: The East Devon Coast between Lyme Regis and Axmouth (11 miles) *The Harbour Inn* 75

13 Ancient Rituals: A Merrivale Circuit (7 miles) *The Dartmoor Inn* 81

14 Where Falcons Fly: Haldon Hill, Doddiscombsleigh and Ashton (7 miles) *The Nobody Inn* 87

15 Uncle Tom Cobley and Other Folk: Widecombe, Hound Tor and Hamel Down (9½ miles) *The Old Inn* 93

16 Monks, Tinners and an Evil Squire: Holne Moor, Buckfast and Hembury Woods (11½ miles) *The Abbey Inn* 99

17 Two Castles: Compton and Berry Pomeroy via Green Lanes (10½ miles) *The Tally Ho Inn* 105

18 Industrial Remains in a Woodland Setting: The Plym Valley (8½ miles) *The White Thorn* 111

19 The Primrose Line: Loddiswell and the Avon Valley (9 miles) *The Loddiswell Inn* 117

20 Literary Memories: Bigbury Bay (9 miles) *The Dolphin Inn* 123

PUBLISHER'S NOTE

We hope that you obtain considerable enjoyment from this book; great care has been taken in its preparation. Although at the time of publication all routes followed public rights of way or permitted paths, diversion orders can be made and permissions withdrawn.

We cannot, of course, be held responsible for such diversion orders and any inaccuracies in the text which result from these or any other changes to the routes nor any damage which might result from walkers trespassing on private property. We are anxious though that all details covering the walks are kept up to date and would therefore welcome information from readers which would be relevant to future editions.

The simple sketch maps that accompany the walks in this book are based on notes made by the author whilst checking out the routes on the ground. However, for the benefit of a proper map, we do recommend that you purchase the relevant Ordnance Survey sheet covering your walk. The Ordnance Survey maps are widely available, especially through booksellers and local newsagents.

Introduction

Why *adventurous* pub walks, you may ask. What constitutes an adventurous walk? Well, adventure can take many forms. It can lie in the sudden appearance of a breathtaking view or the discovery of a beautiful hedgerow, in the fascination of a particular place or the beauty of a whole landscape, in a stolen glimpse of a shy animal or the exploration of a site of historical interest. It may simply be the pleasure of varied scenery or the satisfaction of having overcome a stretch of challenging terrain or mastered a tricky piece of navigation. Or, more likely, it will comprise a mixture of several of these factors.

My aim in putting together this collection of walks has been to introduce you to as wide a range of 'adventurous' experiences as possible. All the routes are from 7 to 12 miles in length (long enough to take in a variety of scenery), all include a pub, and all visit places of interest along the way. But that is all they have in common; otherwise they are as diverse as the landscape of Devon itself. You will walk along disused railways, green lanes, farm paths and barely discernible tracks in open country, among cliffs and heaths, woods and moors, rivers and hills. You will visit historic houses, garden delights, architectural gems, archaeological sites, picturesque villages, places with legendary associations and sites of particular natural interest.

And to add to your enjoyment, each route either starts and finishes near a pub or visits one along the way (or, if you are lucky, both!). These hostelries have been chosen for their situation and atmosphere, as well as the quality of their food and the welcome you will receive, and they are almost as varied as the walks themselves. There are inns that were farmhouses, inns that were cottages, inns that were church houses, inns that were bakeries, inns that were breweries and inns that have always been inns, and they date from the 12th to the 20th centuries.

There are full route descriptions and sketch maps for all the walks, and each section is numbered for ease of reference. The distance of each 'leg' is also provided to help you plan your walk. I have briefly described the places or sights of interest you will see along the way, and related any stories attached to particular sites. There is also a brief outline of what each pub is like. I cannot pretend that these are in any way complete descriptions; they are simply intended to give an idea of the place and what it has to offer.

There is nothing to compare with the satisfaction of sitting at a pretty pub – out in the sun or by a roaring fire – after or during a good, stretching walk and contemplating the adventures you have had and the interesting things you have seen on your day out. I hope you will derive that kind of enjoyment from these walks – I certainly did while I was researching them.

Michael Bennie

ACKNOWLEDGEMENTS

I would like to express my thanks to my two walking companions, Simon McCandlish and Keith Walter, both for their stimulating company and for their comments on what we saw, many of which are incorporated in the descriptions.

Walk 1

THE WRECKERS' COAST: BERRYNARBOR TO ILFRACOMBE

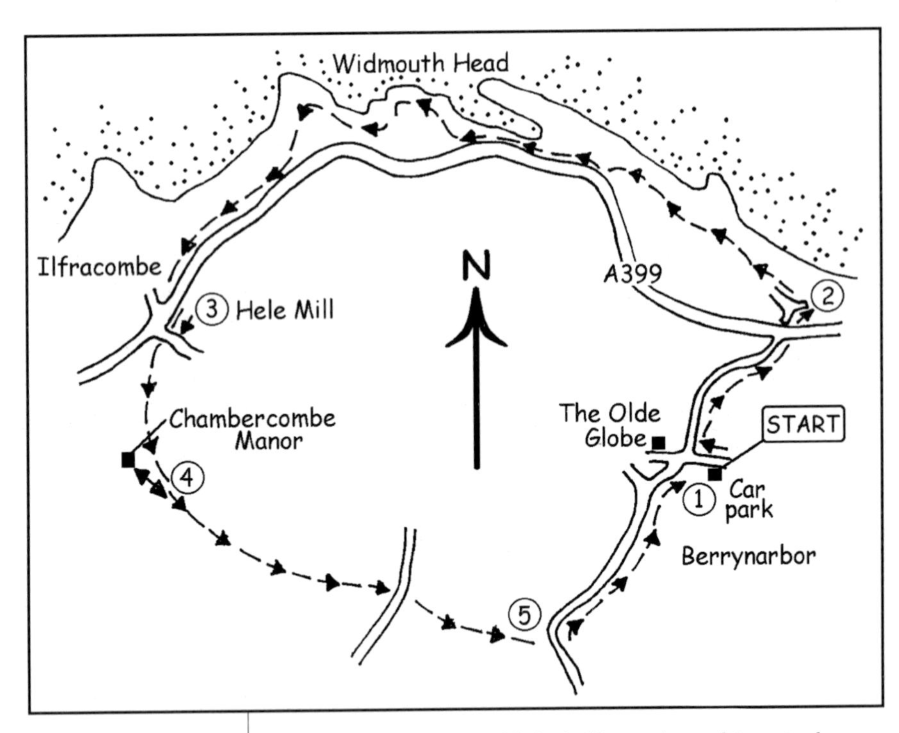

Distance:
7 miles

Starting point:
The free public car park at Berrynarbor, clearly signposted from the centre of the village. GR 561466

Maps: OS Explorer 139 Bideford, Ilfracombe and Barnstaple; OS Explorer OL9 Exmoor; OS Landranger 180 Barnstaple and Ilfracombe

How to get there: *Berrynarbor is just off the A399 to the west of Combe Martin.*

Stunning coastal views are a major feature of this walk. There are one or two stiff climbs to enjoy them, but they are worth the effort. The route follows the South West Coast Path along the top of the cliffs, with treacherous rocks and wild seas below. It then turns inland through the pretty village of Hele, with a chance to visit an old corn mill and the remarkable Chambercombe Manor before returning to Berrynarbor via farm tracks and the gorgeous Sterridge Valley. Some of the tracks can become muddy after rain, so I would advise you to wear appropriate footwear.

The Olde Globe is a delightful old inn, converted from a row of 13th-century cottages which had originally housed masons working on the church. It became a pub in the 17th century, and still has blackened beams, low ceilings and lime ash floors. There is even a well under one of the alcoves.

The main bar is divided into intimate alcoves, and there is also a lounge, a dining room and a family room. Outside there is a lovely garden, with extensive views and a children's play area. Both the lounge and the dining room have large stone fireplaces, with welcoming log fires in winter.

The pub *has a good reputation for its food, which ranges from ploughman's lunches to salads and mouthwatering main courses. Telephone: 01271 882465.*

The Walk

① Turn left as you leave the car park, and at the T-junction turn right to pass the church. Follow the lane out of the village, and when you come to the main road, cross over and follow the Coast Path sign down another lane on the other side. (3/4 mile)

② At the junction at the end, go half left along **Old Coast Road**, following the Coast Path sign again. This takes you above the **Sandy Cove Hotel**. At the end, continue along an unsurfaced track into a wood. This is a lovely stretch, with wild flowers, particularly fine in the spring, and birdsong all around. After a while you leave the wood and get occasional glimpses along the coast through the trees on your right. You pass a caravan site on

THE VIEW TOWARDS STERRIDGE VALLEY

your left, towards the end of which you will see a path going off to the right. This leads you through a gate and into another campsite. Keep to the right-hand boundary as you go down the field and round to the left. Cross a stile and keep to the right in the next field to another stile and a footbridge.

This leads you onto the A399; turn right. After a few yards, bear right to follow the path alongside the road but separated from it by a fence and hedge. You emerge again opposite the entrance to **Watermouth Castle**. After a few yards you have a choice: at low tide you can turn right through a gate and follow the path alongside the water for a short distance until it climbs into the wood alongside; at high tide you have to continue along the road for about 150 yards until you come to a stile on your right. Cross it and bear left along the path through the wood on the other side. You eventually leave the wood and the path turns right to a stile. It goes right again on the other side to round **Widmouth Head**. As you go, you get a good view up **Water Mouth**. There is a steep climb to the top of the headland, but when you get there you will be met by a superb panorama, both back along the coast and ahead. On a clear day, you can also see the coast of Wales across the Bristol Channel. Moreover, there is a convenient seat from which to enjoy it all while you catch your breath.

One of the less savoury occupations of the people of North Devon during the 17th and 18th centuries was the practice of wrecking. This involved shining lights on the headlands along the coast in bad weather to confuse passing ships and lure them onto the rocks below. Any crew or passengers who were not drowned as a result were usually killed by the wreckers, who swarmed onto the stricken vessels and stripped them of anything valuable. As you admire the view from Widmouth Head, you can see how easily a ship could be smashed on this rugged coast.

As you come off **Widmouth Head**, you will find a stile on your right; cross it and skirt round **Samson's Bay**. You emerge onto the road again at a small parking area; turn right and follow the path, which is separated from the road by a small wall. You finally join the road and walk along the verge for 200 yards or so to a car park, where you can join a pavement. (2½ miles)

③ After another 500 yards, as the Coast Path goes right towards the

CHAMBERCOMBE MANOR, ILFRACOMBE

beach, take a public footpath which goes left just beyond a bus stop. This takes you to **Hele Mill**, where you can stop for tea or light refreshments if you fancy a break (alternatively you can wait until you reach **Chambercombe Manor**, where similar refreshments are available when the manor is open).

Hele Mill, a 16th century water-powered corn mill, has been restored and is open to the public, with displays of information and machinery. It sells flour ground on the premises, and there is also pottery for sale (you can even make your own).

Beyond the mill, the path emerges onto a lane; turn right and follow the lane round to the left. When it turns right again, go straight on (signposted to **Littleton, Comyn** and **Trayne**). Take the first turning left (there is a public footpath sign, but it is a little way up the lane). Follow the lane up a hill, and when it turns to the left, go straight on through a gate onto a track. The track comes out at a farm; turn right, and then right again for a short detour to **Chambercombe Manor** (if you do not want to visit the manor, turn right and then left through the farmyard). (1 mile)

The 11th-century Chambercombe Manor once belonged to the family of Lady Jane Grey, who, in 1553, at the age of 15, was made queen in a vain attempt to keep Mary Tudor off the throne. The poor girl lasted just nine days as queen, and was later executed for treason. There is a room in the manor named after her, but there is no evidence that she actually stayed there.

A later occupant was William Oatway, a notorious 18th-century wrecker and smuggler, and a tunnel has been discovered linking the manor with Hele Bay, which was presumably used to bring contraband up from the coast. In 1865, the then tenant was making some repairs when he noticed that there was a blocked-up window with no corresponding room behind it. He took a hammer to the nearest wall and broke through to find that there was a room which had been sealed up, and inside, on a bed, was the skeleton of a woman.

Tradition has it that the woman was Kate Oatway, William's daughter, who had been on one of the ships wrecked by his gang and had been killed. Horrified and filled with remorse, he had carried her body back to Chambercombe and sealed it in her room. It is said that her ghost has haunted the house ever since her remains were disturbed. The house is open for guided tours from Easter to September (telephone 01272 862624 for details).

④ Retrace your steps to **Comyn Farm** and cross the farmyard. At the end, go through a gate on the left and turn immediately right and then left, following the sign to **Trayne** and **Green Park Lane**. Go right up a track alongside a stream. It can become rather muddy after rain, so take care. Where it ends, cross the stream and go through a gate. Follow the grassy track up the field on the other side to a gate, and then across the next field to another gate alongside some farm buildings.

Go through yet another gate into the farmyard and follow the drive on the other side. This brings you out onto a lane. Cross straight over to a footpath sign and stile on the other side. Bear right across the field to another stile and bear right again down the next field. There is a lovely view ahead, across a wooded valley to farm fields. You will find a stile on the right halfway down the field; cross it and the footbridge on the other side, and turn left to follow the path alongside a stream. It can become muddy and overgrown, but is quite passable. Cross another stile and go down the next field. At the end swing left and right to a lane. (1¾ miles)

⑤ Turn left and follow the lane down the lovely **Sterridge Valley**, with a wood on the other side of a stream on your right, and some delightful cottages on your left. At the junction on the outskirts of **Berrynarbor**, turn right (signposted to Berrynarbor and Combe Martin). At the T-junction at the end, turn right to return to the car park or left to reach the **Olde Globe** and quench your thirst. (1 mile)

Date walk completed:

Walk 2

DOONE COUNTRY: NORTH-WESTERN EXMOOR

THE EAST LYN VALLEY

Distance:
12 miles

Starting point:
The National Trust car park at Barna Barrow on the northern side of the road just east of Countisbury. If you are approaching from Countisbury, it is the first turning to the left after you leave the village. GR 753496

Maps: OS Explorer OL9 Exmoor; OS Landranger 180 Barnstaple and Ilfracombe

How to get there: *Countisbury is located on the A39 between Lynmouth and Porlock.*

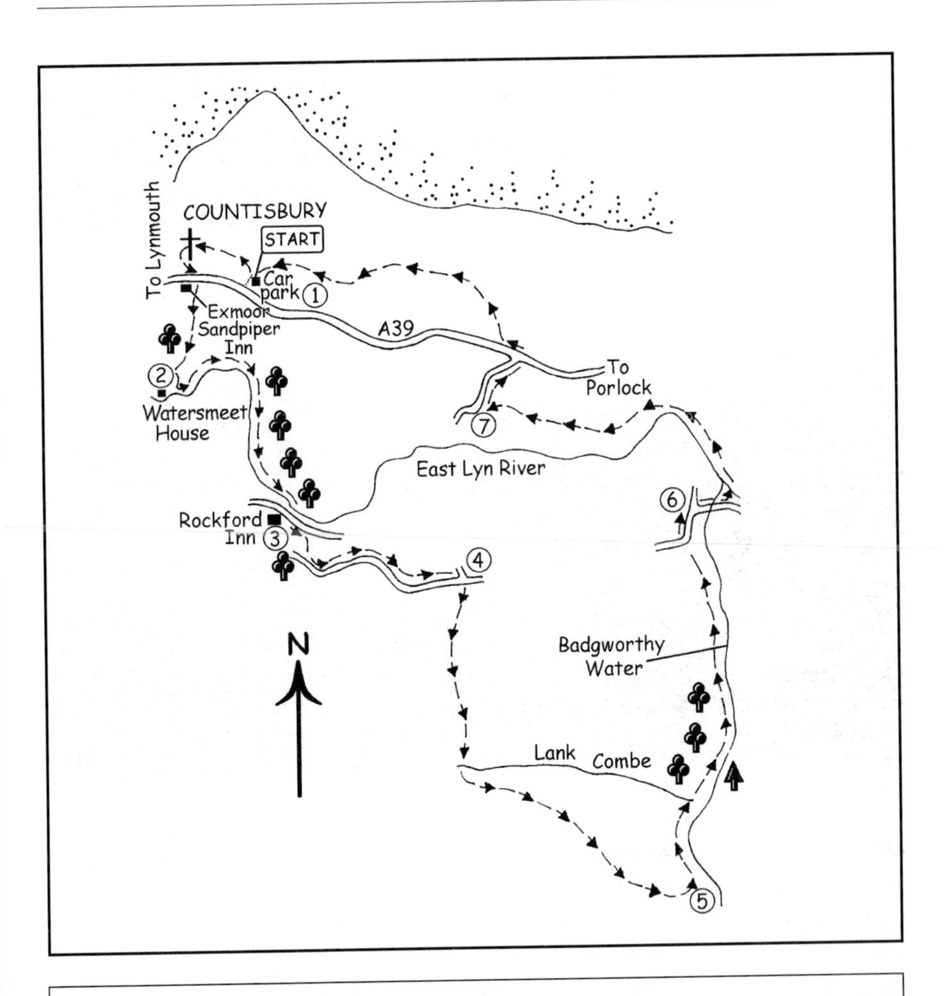

This is a long walk, but for beauty and variety it is hard to beat. It takes in the delightful valley of the East Lyn River – known by the Victorians as the Little Switzerland of England – and the wide open spaces of Exmoor, with its heather-covered slopes and extensive views. This is a wild land of hidden valleys and rugged outcrops, the setting for R.D. Blackmore's classic *Lorna Doone*. There are also some stunning coastal views at the start and towards the end. There are a couple of steep hills to negotiate, but the going is generally fairly easy.

Whoever chose to establish an inn here certainly had an eye for a lovely site. With the river across the lane in front and dense woodland all around, it would be very easy to linger. It is a 17th-century establishment. The accommodation comprises an attractive bar divided in two by a wooden partition, with a wood-burning stove at one end, a delightful lounge with an open fire. Both are furnished with tables, settles and stools, and the lounge also has a very comfortable armchair. There is also a family room at the back and a small patio across the lane in the front. You can tell that you are approaching Doone Country: the bar is called the Carver Doone Bar, and one of the regulars is a gentleman by the name of John Ridd!

It is open *all day from noon on Fridays and Saturdays, but closes in the afternoon on other days. The food is freshly cooked and ranges from soups, ploughman's lunches and salads to steaks, vegetarian meals and wide range of fish. It prides itself on its quality real ales, including its own Rockford Ale. Telephone: 01598 741214.*

The Walk

① Head north along a track from the car park, away from the road. Follow the track round to the left, around a wall. When it forks, keep to the wall. You get some lovely views along the coast, with **Lynton** across the valley ahead. At the end of the wall go half left to a gate into a churchyard. Follow the path round the rather pretty little church and leave the churchyard via another gate. Follow the track on the other side down to the main road. If you fancy some refreshment before you get into the main part of the walk, you will find the **Exmoor Sandpiper Inn** on the other side of the road.

A story is told in Countisbury of a strange occurrence involving a local 'wise woman' known as the white witch of Countisbury. The landlord of the Blue Ball Inn (as the Exmoor Sandpiper was then called) apparently drove a wooden peg through a footprint she had made on her way to church one Sunday. When she tried to rise from her prayers after the service, she found that she was pinned in her place, and the landlord had to remove the peg from her footprint before she could move.

Turn left at the road (right as you leave the Exmoor Sandpiper) and after 50 yards you will see a gate on the right; go through it and follow the grassy track between walls on the other side. Go through another gate and cross a field (signposted to **Watersmeet**). A little way away from the left-hand wall, you will see a post; aim for that and then follow a path beyond it down a hill through the bracken and gorse. Go through a gate and into a delightful wood. The path winds steeply downhill through the wood towards the river, which you can hear and sometimes see through the trees below you. At the bottom, when you come to a sign to **Countisbury** pointing up the path you have just come down, you are faced with a choice: you can go straight on to continue the walk or turn sharp right to reach the National Trust restaurant at **Watersmeet** if you are ready for more refreshment (or just to admire the attractive building and its setting). (1 mile)

Watersmeet House was built in 1832 as a fishing lodge and a more delightful setting for such a building would be hard to find. It has been a tea garden since 1901 and is now owned by the National Trust. There is a shop and a small restaurant where teas, coffees and light meals are served.

② The path takes you high above the **East Lyn River**, and then down until you are walking along the bank. This is a truly idyllic stretch. With the river cascading over the rocks on your right and the lush, green wood all around you, it must be one of the most beautiful valleys in Devon.

After a little over 1/2 mile you will see a footbridge over the river on your right; do not cross it, but continue along the bank (signposted to **Rockford** and **Brendon**). Beyond the bridge the path climbs out of the wood for a while and then re-enters it, and once again you find yourself high above the river. The path descends again, and, 3/4 mile after passing the bridge, you come to a house called **Rockford Lodge**. Go round to the right of it and you will soon see a footbridge on your right. Cross it to a lane and turn left to continue the walk or right for the delightful **Rockford Inn** and an opportunity to replenish your energy reserves for the exertions to come. (1 1/2 miles)

③ Follow the lane up a short hill for about 1/4 mile until you see a long building on your left.

THE ROCKFORD INN, ROCKFORD

Immediately opposite it you will see some steps leading up a bank. The path is not very clear, but at the top of the steps there is a sign pointing to **Brendon Common**. Follow the path up through another lovely wood, with a small stream cascading down on your left. It is not a good idea to over-indulge at the Rockford Inn, as, although this stretch is beautiful, it is also rather steep! It is fairly wet underfoot to begin with, but it dries out as you get higher.

At the top of the hill you emerge onto a lane; turn left. Follow this lane as it winds and climbs (but not nearly as steeply as the path you have just left). From time to time you get some good views across the hedge on your left, and then you come out onto open moorland. About 3/4 mile after joining the lane you will come to a junction, with another lane going off to the left. (1 mile)

④ Turn down a track on the right (signposted to **Dry Bridge** and **Brendon Common**). As you follow it you get a good view ahead over Exmoor. Where the track forks, go straight on, following the line of the bank and hedge on your left. When the bank and hedge turn to the left, go straight on up a hill; as you go, look back for a very good view across the fields towards the coast. Cross another track and then another, much clearer one. Go straight on (signposted to **Doone Valley**). The track crosses a small stream. This is **Lankcombe Ford**, and the valley stretching down to the left is **Lank Combe**, believed to be the basis for R.D. Blackmore's Doone Valley.

Follow the track on the other side of the ford as it swings to the left round the hill. As you do so you get a pleasant view across the heather-clad moorland. The track almost peters out, but you can still see the route, which runs almost parallel with **Lank Combe** on the left, but at a slight angle from it. Do not worry too much if you go slightly wrong, as you can always correct your route when you reach the wall and fence ahead. As you go, enjoy the open spaces and wide skies that are a feature of this part of Exmoor.

As you come over the brow of the hill you get a good view ahead to **Badgworthy Water**. When you reach the wall and fence, go through a gate and continue along the faint but still discernible track that leads down towards the valley you can see ahead of you. It goes slightly right to cross a stream, and then becomes clearer. Where the path forks, go left round the hill, and soon Badgworthy Water comes into view on your right. The name, incidentally, is pronounced 'Badgery', a bit of local knowledge with which you can impress your companions. (2 1/2 miles)

⑤ Follow the path as it runs a little

way above **Badgworthy Water**. After just over 1/4 mile you cross two little streams and find yourself down at the same level as the river, but with a fence between you and it. A little further on there is a gate in the fence, where you can go down to the water if you want to cool your feet or have a picnic, but there will be plenty of other opportunities to do so later on. You enter a stretch of woodland, with a conifer plantation on the right. You are now no longer separated from the river by a fence.

About 1/2 mile after entering the valley of **Badgworthy Water** you cross a footbridge. On your left is **Lank Combe**, and as you look up it it is easy to imagine how it came to be the inspiration for the isolated, rocky valley which hid the Doones' stronghold. Continue along the broad path through the wood, with the river meandering slowly along on your right. If you want to stop for a paddle or a picnic in the shade, there are plenty of places along here. If you prefer sunshine, however, wait until you leave the wood via a gate; there are more spots in the open country beyond.

You pass a memorial to Blackmore on your left and then a campsite on the other side of the river. Pass a footbridge and carry straight on to a gate. Follow the track alongside a wall on the other side to another gate and follow the track between walls. It bends left to cross a stream and goes through yet another gate to a lane. Bear right and follow the lane to a junction. Here you will find **Lorna Doone Farm**, where you can get ice-creams and light refreshments if you still need sustenance. (2 1/4 miles)

⑥ Turn right (signposted to **Oare** and **Porlock**) and cross **Badgworthy Water**. As you do so, you will see that you are passing briefly into **Somerset**. Three hundred yards after crossing the river you will see a public bridleway sign pointing left to **Oare** and **County Gate**. Turn off here and follow the path as it winds to a footbridge. On the other side turn sharp left to follow **Oare Water**. It is lovely along here with the stream on your left and the gorse-, bracken- and heather-covered hill stretching up to your right.

You go through a gate, across a drive and to the left of the house beyond. Cross a stile and continue alongside the river. After a while you cross another stile and the path begins to climb away from the river. It is another steep climb, but you can console yourself with the knowledge that it is the last major climb, and the views across the valley from the top are magnificent.

At the top go through another gate and then go straight on along a clear path that descends and swings to the right and to the left before crossing a footbridge and stile on the right. Follow the path as it contours round the hill. Be careful at the end of this field; do not take the obvious gateway, but go to the left of it, to a stile. Go down some steps and continue along the path as it climbs gently to a gate. On the other side it climbs gently again and you get a gorgeous view down the valley. The hillside on the left is a carpet of yellow gorse and pink heather in late summer, and tormentil and wood sage line the path. Go through two more gates. About 100 yards after the second, as the main path twists to the left, go straight on to join a lane. (1$^3/_4$ miles)

⑦ Turn right, and at the T-junction at the main road turn left. Take care along here as it is a busy road. Follow it for 250 yards to a stile on the right; cross it and keep to the right of the field beyond. As you do so a superb panorama opens up to the right across the coast and the Bristol Channel to Wales. Go through a gate at the end and along a track on the other side, alongside a wall. When it swings to the right, go half left, slightly away from the wall, to a gate. Cross the next field to another gate and bear left to yet another gate, still with the tremendous coastal view on the right.

Cross the next field and pass two gates on your right. Continue along the edge of the field as it curves round to the right and you will reach a track. Turn right, following the sign for **Countisbury**, and after a few yards, as the tracks swings right, go left up a grassy track. When the main track swings round to a gate go straight on to another gate. Cross a surfaced track and continue along the grassy track on the other side (signposted to Countisbury). At the fork go left, and at the next fork left again to return to the car park. (2 miles)

Date walk completed:

Walk 3

STRIP FARMING, SEA SHELLS AND SAND DUNES: BRAUNTON BURROWS TO CROYDE

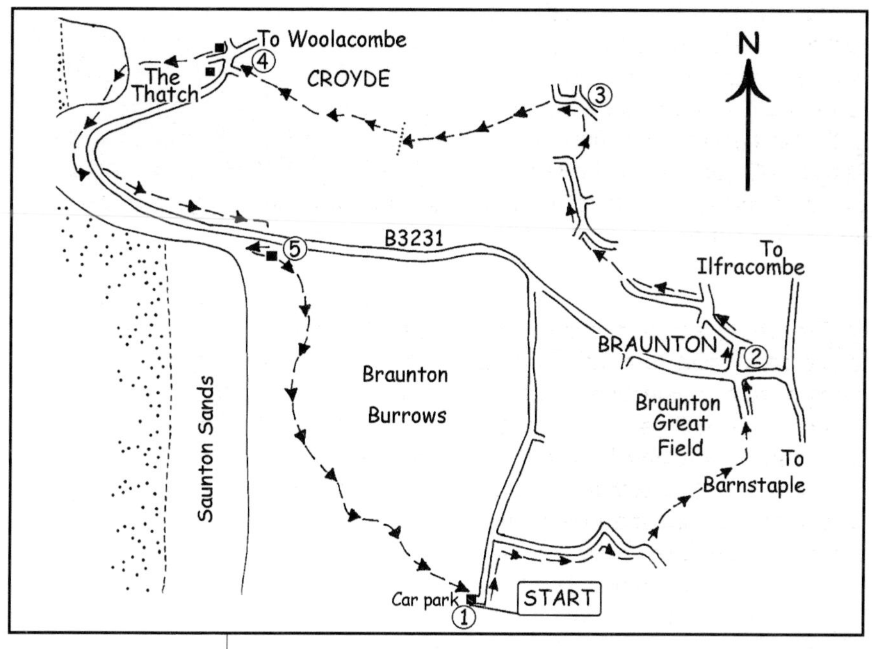

Distance:
$10^1/_2$ miles

Starting point:
Braunton Burrows. There is a car park on the right at the very end of the lane, about $1^1/_2$ miles after leaving the B3231.
GR 463350

Maps: OS Explorer 139 Bideford, Ilfracombe and Barnstaple; OS Landranger 180 Barnstaple and Ilfracombe

How to get there: *Turn west off the A361 Barnstaple to Ilfracombe road at Braunton, onto the B3231 towards Croyde. The second lane on the left after leaving Braunton is signposted to Braunton Burrows.*

CROYDE BAY

The Thatch, in Croyde, is a lovely old establishment whose fame has deservedly spread far beyond the village. It was originally part of St Helen's Priory (now a hotel across the road), although even then it was used by the monks for brewing and storing their beer. Since then it has been a restaurant, a tea-room, even a farm outhouse. It is now a delightful hostelry, with exposed stone walls. The cool, dark bar has low beams and is divided into small, snug alcoves, with a wood-burning stove in the middle. The lounge, which leads off the bar via some steps, is lighter and airier. A separate restaurant and an outdoor patio complete the accommodation.

The food *ranges from soups and snacks such as nachos to a variety of main courses, including steaks and chicken. It also offers a good selection of beers and wines, and is open all day. Telephone: 01271 890349.*

This is a gorgeous walk, combining attractive countryside, beautiful beaches, outstanding views and the widest variety of wild flowers you are likely to come across. There is also a great deal of interest along the way, from a relic of medieval agriculture to one of the largest dune systems in Britain, via a delightful little museum. What is more, it can all be enjoyed without too much effort.

① Turn left as you leave the car park and follow the lane back the way you came. After 1/4 mile, turn right down another lane. As you follow it, look right for a lovely view across the **Taw estuary**. After a little over 1/2 mile, the lane bends sharply to the right and you can see **Braunton Great Field** on your left.

Braunton Great Field is one of the last remaining examples of the system of open-field agriculture which was prevalent across much of lowland England during the Middle Ages.

The lane then swings left. Just as it goes right again, turn left to cross a stile into the Great Field. Bear right alongside the hedge, and when it turns to the right go straight on across the field, following a clear path between the crops.

You join a grassy track; go straight on. At the next two track junctions go straight on again, and at the last one turn right and then left. You will soon find a hedge on your right; keep to the track that runs alongside it and then swings left between hedges. It emerges onto a road on the edge of **Braunton**; go straight on. (2 1/4 miles)

② At the T-junction at the main road, go left and then, after 50 yards or so, turn right up a small lane which seems to be suffering from an identity crisis: the sign you can see from this side seems to suggest that it is called **St Annes Pixie Lane**, while the sign on the other side says it is **Sharlands Lane** (its correct name). Follow it up a hill for about 250 yards to a T-junction; turn left. Stop at the next T-junction and look over to your left for a lovely view across the Taw estuary. Then turn right and after 50 yards left down a lane marked with a 'No through road' sign.

This lane skirts the edge of **Braunton**, with houses on the left and fields on the right. After 600 yards it ends at a private drive for **Fairlinch Farm**, which goes off to the right. As it does so, cross the stile almost straight ahead and bear right across the field beyond. As you cross, you can see **Braunton Burrows** below and slightly behind you to the left, while immediately to the left lies the open sea. In the far corner of the field, you cross another stile into a green lane; as you follow it you continue to get a good view to the left, across **Braunton Burrows** and the Taw estuary and out to sea.

You emerge onto a surfaced lane; go left. At the next two junctions go straight on. The lane climbs gently and at the top of the climb it swings left to a farm; go right along a green lane. This climbs some more and then, just before you reach a gate into a field, it swings left, still climbing. Pause at the top of the hill for your best view yet, over **Saunton Sands** to the left. ($1^3/_4$ miles)

③ You come out at another surfaced lane; bear left and then turn left almost immediately down another lane. When that swings right after 150 yards, go straight on along another green lane. You continue to get glimpses of the outlook across the **Taw estuary** through gateways and across the hedge on your left. You pass an MoD radio mast on your left, and then another on your right.

After about $^3/_4$ mile you will come to a T-junction; turn right (signposted to **Forda**) and then left through a gate (signposted to **Croyde**). Turn right and at the bottom of the field follow the edge round to the left. At the end, cross a stile. As you do so, a whole new vista opens up ahead over **Croyde Bay**. This should give you encouragement, because at the bottom of the hill lies **Croyde village** and the watering hole you have been dreaming about ever since climbing **Lobb Hill**. Go straight across the next field to a stile and follow the footpath on the other side between two fences. This leads you to a track; turn right. At the junction follow the main track down the hill (signposted to **Croyde**). It joins a lane, which takes you down into **Croyde**. Follow this lane right

THE THATCH, CROYDE

down to the main road, and you will find **The Thatch** just across the road on your left. (2 miles)

④ To resume the walk, turn left from The Thatch (right from the lane if you decide not to stop). Follow the main road for about 50 yards, and turn left between **Billy Budd's** restaurant and the **Gem, Rock and Shell Museum**.

The Gem, Rock and Shell Museum has an interesting exhibition of semi-precious stones from around the world, both in their natural state and cut and polished. There is also an interesting display of the world's seashells. It is open from March to October (telephone 01271 890671 for details).

At the end of the lane, continue along a footpath, which leads to an open field. Cross the field to a gate and then follow the left-hand path, which takes you between wooden fences to the sand dunes of **Croyde Burrows**. Go straight on, following a row of yellow-topped posts, over the dunes to the beach. Turn left along the top of the beach (or go down to the water if you would like to cool your feet with a paddle).

At the end of the beach, go up a path and some steps that climb up the side of the rocks. At the top turn right (signposted for the **Coast Path** and the **Tarka Trail** to **Braunton**). Follow the path round above the rocks, noticing the interesting formations as you go. Look out to your right and you will see the island of **Lundy**, with the coast stretching away beyond the **Taw estuary** half right.

After about 600 yards you go through a kissing-gate. Turn left and left again to climb up away from the rocks, with a lovely view across **Saunton Sands** as you do so. You come out at a road; turn left and follow the road (carefully, as it is busy, especially in summer) for about 50 yards. Then turn right up some steps and right again, following the Coast Path sign. You are now walking above the road, and you get an even more spectacular view across **Saunton Sands** and **Braunton Burrows** to **Appledore** on the other side of the estuary.

After a mile the path descends to the road. Cross with care and follow the path on the other side to the left of the **Saunton Sands Hotel**. At the bottom go right and through a gate. Continue along the front of the hotel and then follow the path as it winds down to the public car park below. (2 miles)

⑤ Turn left and aim for the far right-hand corner. A short path leads from there across a dune to another car park. Keep to the right of that to reach another path, which takes you onto the dunes of **Braunton Burrows**.

Braunton Burrows National Nature Reserve comprises one of the largest sand-dune systems in Britain. There are over 4 square miles of them running inland from the magnificent 4-mile stretch of Saunton Sands, and they are home to over 400 species of flowering plants, as well as a wide variety of mammals, birds and insects. You can usually wander through the dunes at will, but the southern part of the reserve is a military training area, so you should look out for the red flags that indicate that firing is taking place, and not enter the danger area (indicated by red and white posts).

You will find minor paths leading off to the right and left, but you should keep to the main one, which is clearly distinguishable. Having said that, it doesn't matter too much if you do stray – if you go too far to the right you will find yourself on the beach, and if you go too far to the left you will come to a golf course. Either way, you need only turn back to the central path. So just wander along admiring the stunning variety of wild flowers on either side.

After a short distance you will find one of the greens of the golf course on your left. This is not because you have strayed from the path; it simply juts out from the main course. You will eventually come to a fenced area; follow the path round to the right and then to the left to circumvent it. Do the same again some distance later, when you come to another fenced area.

About a mile after entering the dune system, you will come to a track. Turn left along it. At this point you will also see some red and white posts alongside the track, indicating the beginning of the military area. You should not leave the track if there are red flags flying from the dunes above. When the track forks, go left. After 1/4 mile you will find a fence on your left; follow it for about 200 yards and then the track swings away from it to the right. After another 150 yards it swings left again and runs for about 1/2 mile, with only minor twists, straight back to the car park. (2 1/2 miles)

Date walk completed:

Walk 4

SHIPWRECKS AND SAINTS: DEVON'S WEST COAST

THE VIEW FROM BLEGBERRY CLIFF

Distance:
$9^1/_4$ miles

Starting point:
The car park at Hartland Point. GR 235275

Maps: OS Explorer 126 Clovelly and Hartland; OS Landranger 190 Bude and Clovelly

How to get there: *Take the B3248 from the A39 Bideford to Bude road towards Hartland, and follow the signs for Hartland Point.*

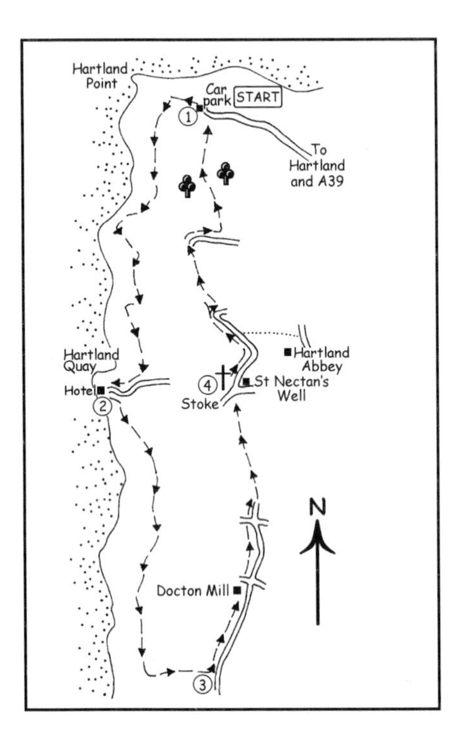

This is a marvellous walk, with a great variety of scenery and some magnificent views. It follows the South West Coast Path along Devon's Atlantic coast, renowned for the number of ships wrecked there, returning along flower-filled green lanes. There is a great deal to see along the way, including a museum of shipwrecks, a beautifully restored mill and garden, the well of a Celtic saint and, with a slight detour, a 12th-century abbey. There are some steep hills to climb on the way, both along the coast and on the return leg, but the effort is well worthwhile.

The 16th-century Hartland Quay Hotel is part of the old quay. It was converted into a hotel at the end of the 19th century. The main bar is called the Wreckers' Retreat, in recognition of the unsavoury activities of some of the locals in bygone times. It is a long room, with wooden panelling and bench seats, decorated with pictures and memorabilia of some of the wrecks that have happened along this coast. There are small alcoves, giving the room a warm, cosy atmosphere, and alongside is a light, airy eating area.

The food *is all home cooked, and ranges from soups and ploughman's lunches to steaks, pasta and fish dishes. Telephone: 01237 441218 (for both the hotel and the museum).*

The Walk

① Turn left from the car park, following the clear path. You can see the island of **Lundy** out to sea as you go. The structure you can see on the right of the car park is the dome of a radar station which was built here during the Second World War. You soon come to a surfaced track which leads to the gates of the lighthouse. Take the narrow path which goes up to the left of the gates. When you come to the coastguard station, go right for an excellent view of **Hartland Point** and the lighthouse.

To continue the walk, go back round the coastguard station and then straight on, following the yellow waymark. The path goes to the right and then to the left along the coast. Cross a stile and keep to the right of a field; at the bottom follow the hedge round to the left to another stile. Go left again to follow the outside of the hedge. Cross another stile and go right, alongside another field. The path now descends quite steeply and goes to the left to cross a footbridge. It climbs up the opposite hillside via a series of steps.

At the top, turn right and cross a stile. At the junction go straight on, following the **Coast Path** sign. Cross another stile and go down to a flat meadow. At the end of the meadow turn left to clamber up some rocks and then climb a promontory. At the top you get a breathtaking view along the coast. At the junction at the top of the promontory, go straight on, following the **Coast Path** sign again. Notice the strange rock formations below you.

Go steeply down the other side to a gate and cross another stream. Turn left on the other side, cross a stile and go straight on, still following the **Coast Path** sign. At the top turn right and then left across a stile and then go steeply down the next slope. And the answer to the obvious question at this point is, yes, I am afraid you do have to climb the hill on the other side. But take heart – it does not seem to be quite as steep when you get there as it does from this side, and beyond the hill lies **Hartland Quay** and a refreshment stop!

At the bottom, turn left past a house; just beyond it turn right and go through a kissing gate into a field. Halfway across the field go right across a stile, following the waymark, then go right once again and through a gate. This leads you up the hill, and at the top it levels off. On your left you can see the tower of **Stoke church** and, closer to, the ruin of what is believed to have been a summer house belonging to **Hartland Abbey**. Cross a stile to the right of the house you can see, and turn right along a surfaced path. Where the path goes to the left, go straight on. You join a lane; go straight on again, and you will come out at **Hartland Quay** and its hotel. (2¾ miles)

There is an interesting little museum on the quay, which records its history and the

geology and natural history of the area, as well as the stories of the many wrecks along this stretch of coast and tales of smugglers and coasters. It is open from June to September. There is also a shop selling souvenirs, ice-creams, etc.

② Do not take the lane up from **Hartland Quay**, but turn right from the car park, up some steps, following the **Coast Path** waymark. You go through a gate and follow the clear path on the other side. After a while you go through another gate into a field. Cross a stream via some stepping stones and bear left to another gate; turn right on the other side, and follow a path up a hill to the left. At the top you cross a ladder stile and start going steeply down. Be careful as you go, because although there are steps it is fairly slippery.

At the bottom of the hill you meet a track; turn left. After a short distance turn right, following the **Coast Path** sign, and cross a footbridge. On the other side you have a choice: you can either go right along the clifftop or left around the valley. My suggestion would be to take the valley route – there is still quite a long way to go, including some steep hills, and you might be advised to conserve your energy.

After following the valley route for 1/4 mile, you will come to a signpost, showing the **Coast Path** going right. It is hidden by a hedge, however, so look out for it. If you reach a stream, then you will know that you have gone too far. The path runs up the valley, slightly above the stream. Towards the top, you will find a gate on your right; take the path that runs up to the

THE HARTLAND QUAY HOTEL

right of it. You cross a stile on your left, and this is where the cliff path rejoins your route.

Continue along the top of the cliff, crossing another stile as you go, and about 1/2 mile after leaving the valley and linking up with the cliff path, you will come to a public footpath sign pointing left across a stile to **Elmscott**. Cross that stile and keep to the right of the field on the other side of the stile. At the end, follow the hedge round to the left; as you go, you can see **Lundy Island** again out to sea half-left and the radar dome at **Hartland Point** ahead of you. This will remain in view for most of the rest of the walk, as a beacon beckoning you onward. Halfway along the field you will find a stile on your right; cross it and follow the track on the other side. (2 1/2 miles)

③ The track comes out at a lane; turn left. At the junction go straight on (signposted to **Stoke** and **Hartland**). It is a quiet, pretty lane with a mass of wild flowers alongside and birds in the hedges. After a little over 1/2 mile you will find **Docton Mill** on your left; if you feel in need of further refreshment, there are light lunches, cream teas etc on offer here.

Docton Mill dates back to Saxon times, and only stopped working in 1910. Its main attraction is the garden, which runs down the Speke Valley and up the slopes on either side. There are several attractions, including a wide collection of narcissi in spring, a bog garden, a golden dry garden and a superb collection of magnolias. It is open from March to October (telephone 01237 441369 for details).

At the crossroads just beyond **Docton Mill** go straight on (signposted to **Stoke** and **Hartland** again). You go up a hill alongside a stream; it is quite a steep climb but pretty. At the next crossroads, go straight on again, down a lane marked as unsuitable for motors. Just before you reach a farmyard, turn left along a green lane. It takes you down a hill and across a stream, before climbing steeply up another hill. At the junction at the top, go straight on into the hamlet of **Stoke**. Turn right at the T-junction and follow the lane for about 50 yards to a path on the left if you want to visit **St Nectan's well**, or turn left to visit the church and continue the walk. (2 miles)

St Nectan was a 6th-century Welsh missionary who settled first in Newlyn, Cornwall, and then moved north to Stoke, preaching the Christian gospel. His well is still there, about 100 yards from the church which is dedicated to him. The church was founded by Gytha, wife of the Saxon Earl

Godwin and mother of King Harold, in gratitude for her husband's survival after being shipwrecked on the coast. The present church is 15th-century.

④ At the church turn right down a lane marked as unsuitable for motors. Follow it down to cross the **Abbey River** and climb the hill on the other side. The large house you can see on your right on the other side is **Hartland Abbey**, but there is no public access from this side. To visit it you will have to make a detour of about a mile. At the top of the hill you will find a public footpath sign pointing through a gate on the right; to visit the abbey, take that path, and where it joins another lane, turn right.

Hartland Abbey was founded in the 12th century as an Augustinian house, but became a private residence at the Dissolution of the Monasteries in the 16th century. It is now open to the public on certain days during the summer (telephone 01237 441264 for details).

As you reach the top of the hill, you get a good view across the valley to **Stoke** on your left, with the summer house you passed on the way out half-left. The lane goes through a farmyard and swings to the right. As it does so, turn off left down another green lane, marked as unsuitable for motor vehicles. It runs down into a valley (take care, as it can become a bit muddy at times), and then climbs out again. Just before a farm you come to a fork; go right to join a surfaced lane. At the end, go right and after about 250 yards you will come to a turning on the left, signposted 'To the public bridleway'. Leave the lane at this turning and turn left again before a gate to join another green lane. You get a very attractive view across the valley to a patchwork of farms and hedges, with the radar dome and the coastguard station ahead.

Go down into another valley and a delightful little wood. Cross a footbridge, go through a gate and cross another stream. At the T-junction turn right and follow a track up to a farm. Go through a gate and cross the farmyard to a concrete drive. At the top of the drive go straight on and follow a tarred road back to the car park. (2 miles)

Walk 5

WIDE SKIES AND OPEN SPACES: EXMOOR'S SOUTHERN FRINGE

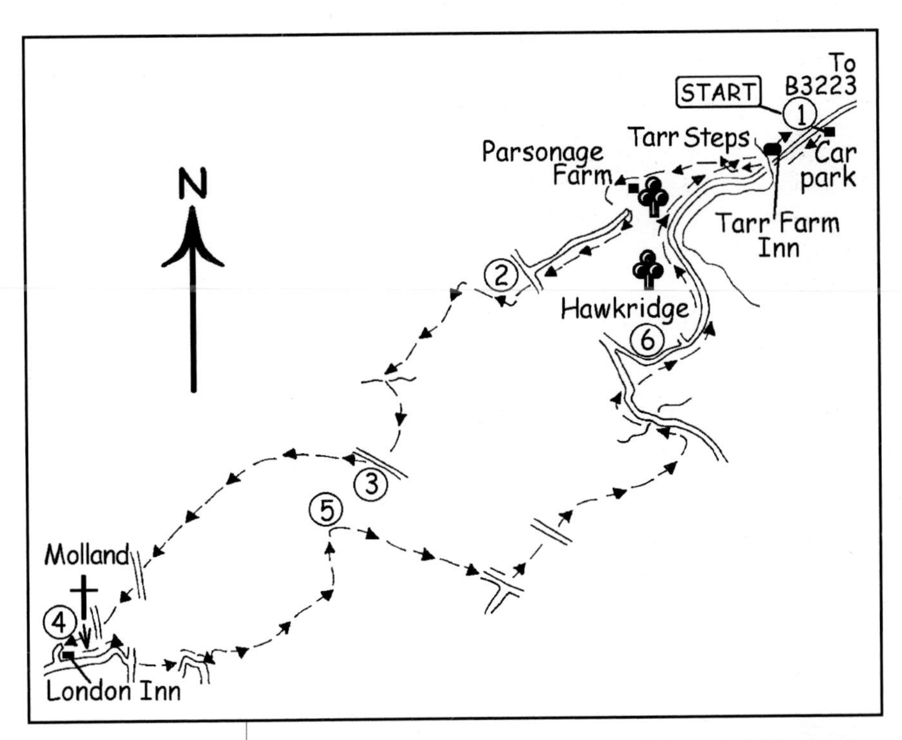

Distance:
12 miles

Starting point:
Tarr Steps. There is a large public car park on the left about 500 yards before you reach the Steps. GR 872323

Maps: OS Explorer OL9 Exmoor; OS Landranger 181 Minehead and the Brendon Hills

How to get there: *Tarr Steps is a little over a mile west of the B3223 between Dulverton and Simonsbath, and clearly signposted from that road.*

The peaceful woods fringing the River Barle, the patchwork fields of the upland farms, the open spaces and almost tangible silence of the moors and the picturesque villages of Molland and Hawkridge – this superb walk includes them all and more, enabling you to experience the rich variety of landscapes that Exmoor has to offer. And although there are a few stiff climbs to negotiate, the views more than make up for the effort. (Note: This walk starts and finishes in Somerset, but the bulk of it is in Devon.)

The London Inn, in Molland, halfway round the route, is a gem of a pub. It is a 15th-century coaching inn with many of its original features: dark beams, little nooks, exposed walls, wooden panels and log fires in winter. The entrance is through a porch, which leads into an attractive lounge with a hatch into the bar. The latter is a delightful little room off to the left and beyond that is a cosy family lounge. To the right of the main lounge is a spacious restaurant. There is also a pleasant beer garden outside.

The whole place is beautifully and sympathetically decorated, with comfortable seats and sporting prints.

The food *is based on local produce where possible, and is all home made. The menu ranges from ploughman's lunches and jacket potatoes to steak and fish main courses. There is a separate evening menu. Telephone: 01769 550269.*

① Leave the car park at the bottom end, following the sign pointing to the scenic path to **Tarr Steps**. Go through a gate and swing left to go round a field. Go down some steps and across a footbridge. Go through another gate on the right and follow a path alongside a stream. At the bottom go through a kissing gate onto a track; turn right, cross another footbridge and bear left to **Tarr Steps**.

The medieval clapper bridge called Tarr Steps crosses the River Barle (some 55 feet wide at this point) in seventeen spans of flat stones, the largest of which is over 8 feet long and 5 feet wide, and weighs 2 tons.

Cross the clapper bridge and a few yards up the road beyond bear right up a surfaced track (signposted as the **Two Moors Way** to **Withypool Hill** and **Hawkridge**). When you come to a gate leading to a drive, bear right up a path. This climbs steeply through a pretty wooded area, broadening as it goes. Go through a gate and swing right; when you come to the next gateway, turn left just before it to follow the side of the field, with a hedge on your right. Go through a gate and keep to the left of the next field. Look over to the right for a good view over the farmland. Go through another gate and keep to the left of the next field. At the end go through yet another gate (signposted to **Hawkridge**). Follow a track to another gate and turn right, or go through the gate to **Parsonage Farm** if you are already feeling the need for some refreshment – but bear in mind that you have only covered a mile so far, so it is as well not to linger too long!

Follow the track round to the left and down a hill; it turns sharply to the left to cross a bridge and then sharply left again to climb out of the valley. You come out at a lane; turn right and follow the lane to a T-junction; turn left. (2 miles)

② After a few yards turn right down a track. The outlook ahead of you as you do so is particularly fine. The track goes to the left; when you come to a gateway in a hedge, do not go through it, but turn right through another gate into a field. Keep to the left until you come to a gate on the left; go through it and turn right through another gate to continue along the other side of the hedge. You now get another good view of the patchwork of fields across the valley on your left and ahead. At the end of the field go round to the left (there is a signpost pointing to **Lyshwell**, although there is nowhere else to go anyway; and just to reinforce the message there is a blue-topped post halfway down the field to indicate the way).

The path takes you along the top of a steep-sided valley. You come to a fingerpost pointing to **Anstey Gate**; follow its direction and you will come to a track, where you should turn right. At the bottom cross a footbridge and climb up through the gorse on the other side. Continue along the side of a hill to a yellow-topped post; bear left at the track just beyond it and follow that up the hill to two gates in the far corner of the field.

Take the left gate and turn left beyond it to reach another yellow-topped post and another track. Follow the track down to the right, through a gate and down to a stream. It turns sharply to the left up the other side of the valley. There is a steep climb, but when you get to the top there is a delightful vista up the valley on your left, and also across it behind you. The track swings to the right at the top and you go through another gate. There is another short climb on the other side, but when you come to the top you are rewarded by the most stunning panorama ahead, all the way to the tors of Dartmoor. (1 1/2 miles)

③ You come to a road; cross it to a car park and bear right, following the direction of the bridleway sign pointing to **Molland**. You will find two gaps on the right of the car park; take the second one to a rough grassy track which leads at an angle away from the road. This is a gorgeous stretch: you continue to enjoy the magnificent view over to the left to Dartmoor while you cross the heather-covered moorland (a mass of purple in late summer), with the sky a vast dome above you. This is Exmoor at its best.

You will cross different tracks going off to left and right; ignore them and keep to the one you are on, across the top of a small valley. When you come to a fork, however, after about 1/2 mile or so, take the broader track round to the left. The tracks are not always quite clear – sometimes they are little more than breaks in the bracken and heather – but they are always discernible. You cross another, much clearer, track, and on the other side you will find that your own track becomes clearer. The purple of the heather is now interspersed with the yellow of gorse.

The path becomes less clear again, but as long as you keep to the top of the valley on your right, you will be able to pick it up later as it becomes more marked again. It now descends into a valley to a gate. Follow the track on the other side (marked as an unmetalled road). At the end you come to a road. Cross over to a gate and bear left, following the public footpath sign. At the corner of the hedge go down to cross a footbridge and a stile. Bear left on the other side, following a broad grassy track which contours up the hill to a gate leading into a lane.

Cross the lane to another gate and bear left, again following the public footpath sign. Go through another gate in the far corner of the field and go diagonally across the next field to a third gate. Pass the farm the other side to reach a lane on the edge of the picturesque village of **Molland**. Follow the lane round to the left and at the end turn left to reach the **London Inn** and a well-earned (and no doubt welcome) drink. (2 miles)

④ Turn left outside the pub and you will pass the church on your left. This is worth a slight detour up some steps to visit.

Built in the 15th and 16th centuries, Molland church is one of the few not to have been 'improved' by the Victorians, and

retains its Georgian atmosphere, with whitewashed walls, box pews and a three-decker pulpit. Also notice the folding gates in the quasi-screen.

At the junction outside the village, go straight on. At the next junction go straight on again, up a track and through a gate. Keep to the right of the field beyond to another gate and to the right of the next field to yet another gate. Make your way across the next field, winding down a steep hill among the bracken. You will find a stile in the fence at the bottom, just a few yards to the right of a bend in the lane beyond. Cross it and turn left, following the lane round to the right. It crosses a stream and climbs steeply up the other side of the valley, swinging to the right as it does so.

When the lane bends sharply to the right, go straight on (signposted to **Gourte Farm**).

At the fork go left. Cross a cattle grid and follow the surfaced track up the hill to the right and through a gate. When it swings left to a farmyard go straight on along an unsurfaced track, still climbing. It passes through another gate at the top of the hill and swings to the left. You can now once again enjoy the magnificent view across to Dartmoor, this time on your right.

At the end of the next field there are two gates; go through the right-hand one, which leads into a conifer plantation. At the next fork go right, following the public bridleway sign. At the bottom go straight on across a footbridge and through a gate into a broadleaved wood. At the next junction go straight on and you come to a house. Go straight on up a track to the left of the house. At the top of the climb, follow the track round to the left and through a gate. It goes right to another gate and then straight on to a cattle grid. (3 miles)

⑤ You are now back on open moorland. Turn right along the track; there is a sign pointing to **West Anstey**, but at the time of writing, it had come off the post. Cross a cattle grid and go through a gate, and continue along the track on the other side. You join a surfaced lane; go straight on until you come to a junction. Here you will find a

ST MARY'S CHURCH, MOLLAND

wooden sign pointing left off the lane to **Hawkridge**. This path will take you to a track which goes to the right; follow that, pausing from time to time to look back at the view of Dartmoor behind you. You cross another track and continue to a road.

Cross the road (still signposted to **Hawkridge**). The path is no longer very easy to see, but soon you will come across a much clearer one bearing right; follow that as it skirts round the hill. The path leads to another road; turn left and follow it down a steep hill to cross the brook.

Unfortunately what goes down must come up, and there is an equally steep hill to climb on the other side. Fortunately it is only about $^{1}/_{4}$ mile or so. You will find that the lane bends to the right and then to the left. Just as it goes to the left, go straight on through a gate. There is a sign indicating the **Two Moors Way**, but it is somewhat buried in the hedge. Cross the field on the other side to another gate in the far left-hand corner, which leads into a lane. ($1^{3}/_{4}$ miles)

⑥ Bear right into **Hawkridge** and take comfort from the fact that you are on the last leg, and there is no more difficult climbing before the next hostelry. Follow the lane as it winds through the village. At the junction at the end, by the church, go straight on (signposted to **Tarr Steps**) and then follow the lane to the left. It descends steeply and enters a delightful wood by the **River Barle**. This lovely stretch lasts for $^{1}/_{2}$ mile, with a thickly wooded hill on the left and the river flowing gently on the right. The lane then leaves the river, as the latter swings to the right, only to rejoin it just over $^{1}/_{4}$ mile further on, back at **Tarr Steps**. Cross the clapper bridge, and you will find the **Tarr Farm Inn** a few yards up the road on the left if you are ready for some more refreshment. You can return to the car park along the scenic path you used on the way out. The lane is somewhat easier and a bit shorter, however, with a gentler climb, and therefore perhaps more suitable for the end of the walk! ($1^{3}/_{4}$ miles)

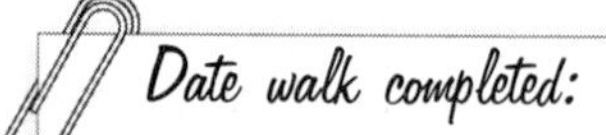

IN THE FOOTSTEPS OF THE OTTER: THE TARKA TRAIL AT TORRINGTON

THE CLINTON ARMS, FRITHELSTOCK

Distance:
10½ miles

Starting point:
The car park described opposite. GR 486195

Maps: OS Explorer 126 Clovelly and Hartland; OS Landranger 180 Barnstaple and Ilfracombe

How to get there: *Great Torrington is on the A386 between Okehampton and Bideford. The car park is on the western edge of the town. If you are approaching from the Bideford direction, go past the sign for the Tarka Trail and park in the next car park on the left. There are actually two car parks: one just off the road and the other further down a track on the right. The walk description starts at the latter.*

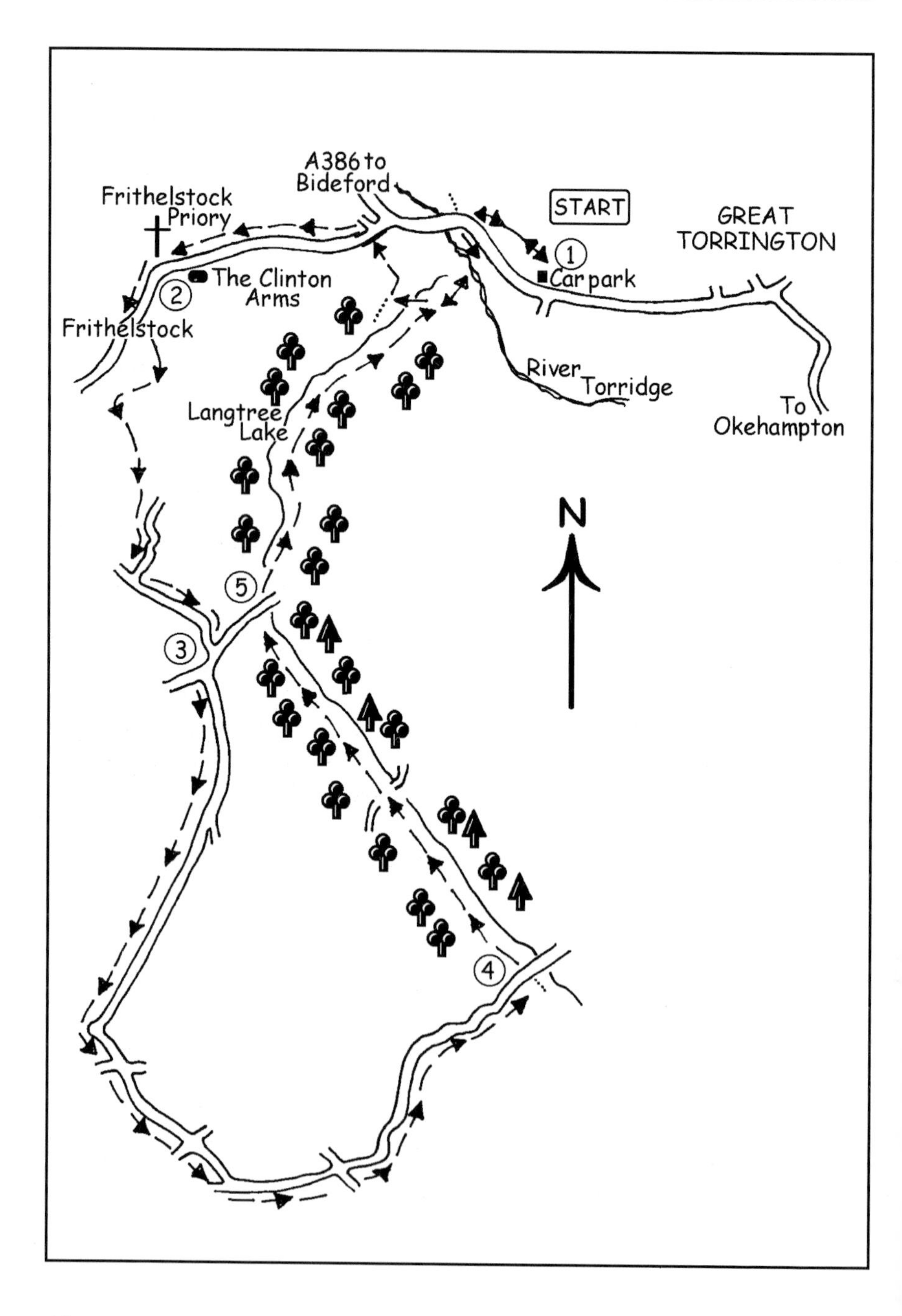
A386 to
Bideford
Frithelstock
Priory
START
GREAT
TORRINGTON
1
Car park
2
The Clinton
Arms
Frithelstock
River
Torridge
To
Okehampton
Langtree
Lake
N
5
3
4

This is a lovely walk at any time, but it comes into its own particularly in spring and summer, when the lanes and tracks are ablaze with flowers; and despite its length it is not difficult – there is not much climbing, and what there is is not unduly strenuous. Most of the outward route follows hardly used lanes and farm paths, and you return through woodland along the gorgeous Tarka Trail.

Great Torrington was the scene of the last major battle of the English Civil War, and although this walk avoids the town itself, it is worth visiting the Torrington 1646 Heritage Centre in the town centre while you are here. It tells the story of the battle that raged through Torrington's streets on that February night, and of the struggle for dominance of the town that preceded it.

The Clinton Arms, in Frithelstock, halfway round the walk, is a welcoming hostelry that is considerably more modern than it looks. It was built to replace an earlier inn, which burned down in 1945, but has the charm and atmosphere of a much older establishment. The accommodation comprises a delightful bar, a snug lounge with deep armchairs, a pleasant restaurant and a lovely walled garden. Also, there are tables out on the village green.

The pub *has its own Clinton Ale, brewed for it by a local Torrington brewery. The delicious food is home made, using local produce wherever possible, and ranges from soup and filled baguettes to mouthwatering pasta dishes and pies. Telephone: 01805 623279.*

The Walk

① Leave the car park at the northern end, furthest from the road, and turn left along **Alexander Path**. You immediately get a good view across the valley as the path skirts the top of **Torrington Common**, with large patches of rosebay willowherb alongside in summer.

When the path forks, go left to reach the A386. Turn right along the road to cross a bridge over the dismantled railway that forms the **Tarka Trail** along this stretch, and on the other side turn left along a track, following a public footpath sign. After a few yards turn left along a path and under an arch. On the other side turn right onto the **Tarka Trail**.

You cross a long steel bridge and enter a wood. Cross a farm track and soon you will go through a narrow gap alongside a gate. A few yards beyond that turn right through another gate to leave the Trail, following the public bridleway sign. Cross a footbridge and keep to the left of the field beyond to yet another gate. Follow the path on the other side to a drive and turn sharp right. The drive leads to a track, which meets a road after about 500 yards; turn left. The road climbs steadily for a little more than 1/2 mile to **Frithelstock**, with a good view to the right as it does so. In the centre of the village, alongside the green, you will find the **Clinton Arms** on your left, ready to provide the refreshment you need to continue the walk, and the church, with the ruins of **Frithelstock Priory** alongside, on the right. (1 3/4 miles)

A WOOD CARVING ALONG THE TARKA TRAIL

The Augustinian Frithelstock Priory was established by Sir Robert de Bello Campo in 1229 to ensure that there would be someone to pray for his soul for ever after his death. The ruins to the north-east of the present church are those of the west front of the monastic church, while the earthworks further north are probably the remains of the cloisters. The present church is believed to have been built at about the same time, probably for the priory's retainers and the villagers who served it.

② Continue through the village, and about 1/4 mile after leaving the pub leave the road via a gate on the left just before a house, following the public footpath sign. Go straight up the field, pausing as you do so to catch your breath and admire the view over the rolling farmland behind you. Cross a stile in the hedge at the top and turn right to follow the edge of the field. At the end, follow the hedge round to the left, and when it goes off to the right, go straight on. You join a track; follow it round to the left, and after a few yards turn right to leave it, following the footpath sign. Follow the edge of the field round to the left. You now get an attractive view to the left.

You join another track; bear left and follow it through a gate into a lane. Turn right. It winds past some houses to a T-junction; turn left. You now get the best view so far, first to the right and after a little while to the left as well. The lane descends steeply and winds past a farm to a road. (1¾ miles)

③ Turn right and after a few yards left (signposted to **Peters Marland** and **Shebbear**). Follow this lane into pretty woodland, with a stream bubbling along on your right. After about ½ mile you will come to a junction; turn right (signposted to **Collacott**). This lane continues to follow the stream and then leaves it to climb steeply out of the valley. After ¾ mile it turns sharply to the left, and passes some buildings. At the junction just beyond them go straight on (signposted to **Peters Marland** and **Shebbear**). A hundred yards further on there is another junction; go straight on again.

The lane continues for 600 yards to a crossroads; go straight on (signposted to **Peters Marland**). At the T-junction at the end turn left. After another 600 yards you come to another crossroads; go straight on (signposted to **Stowford**). Follow this lane as it winds to the left, then to the right and then to the left again. You get a lovely view as you go, of the farms and woods across the valley ahead. After ¾ mile you pass some houses and the lane descends into the valley and enters a wood. (3½ miles)

④ Turn left through a gate to rejoin the **Tarka Trail**. You can now relax in the knowledge that the rest of the walk, apart from a short, easy climb at the end, is along this smooth, level track. And if you are looking for somewhere for a picnic lunch, this is the place to stop. The Trail runs through a beautiful wood, in summer initially fringed by rosebay willowherb, and then by a wide variety of other flowers: enchanter's nightshade, meadowsweet, red campion, hedge woundwort and a host of others.

The Tarka Trail is a long-distance route that links most of the places mentioned in Henry Williamson's classic* Tarka the Otter*. It covers some 180 miles, and takes in the whole of 'the 'Country of the Two Rivers', as it is called in the book – the two rivers being the Taw and the Torridge.

This stretch of the Trail follows the track of the dismantled railway that served the Marland clay quarries along Langtree Lake and one of its tributaries. It also carried passengers, as well as milk from the surrounding farms. The area seems to have changed little

since Williamson wrote about Tarka and his family coming up here on their way to Merton Moors. It was along here that Iggiwick, the hedgehog, was killed by a badger.

You enter a stretch of dense woodland, with the trees forming an arch overhead and the stream winding along way below you on the right. After 3/4 mile you cross a bridge over a lane, and after another 3/4 mile you emerge through a gate into a car park. (1 1/2 miles)

⑤ Cross the road beyond the car park and bear right to rejoin the **Tarka Trail**. Soon after doing so you will see a platform on your left. This is all that remains of **Watergate Halt**, where passengers boarded the train and milk was loaded for transportation to Torrington and on to London. You now have **Langtree Lake** on your right, but the water soon passes under you and continues its journey on the left. Your route continues to be lined with meadowsweet in summer, as well as nipplewort and broad-leaved willowherb among many others, and in spring by a carpet of bluebells.

About 1 1/4 miles after crossing the road at **Watergate** you will find yourself on familiar ground as you go through a gap alongside a gate – this is the route you followed on the way out. Cross the **River Torridge** again and on the other side turn left off the **Tarka Trail**, following the sign for **Taddiport** and **Great Torrington**. Go under the arch and turn right onto the track. At the road turn right to cross the Trail and then left onto **Torrington Common**. At the fork go right onto **Alexander Path** and follow it back to the car park. (2 miles)

Date walk completed:

Walk 7

THE ENGINEERS AND THE ECCENTRIC: THE GRAND WESTERN CANAL AND THE EXE VALLEY WAY

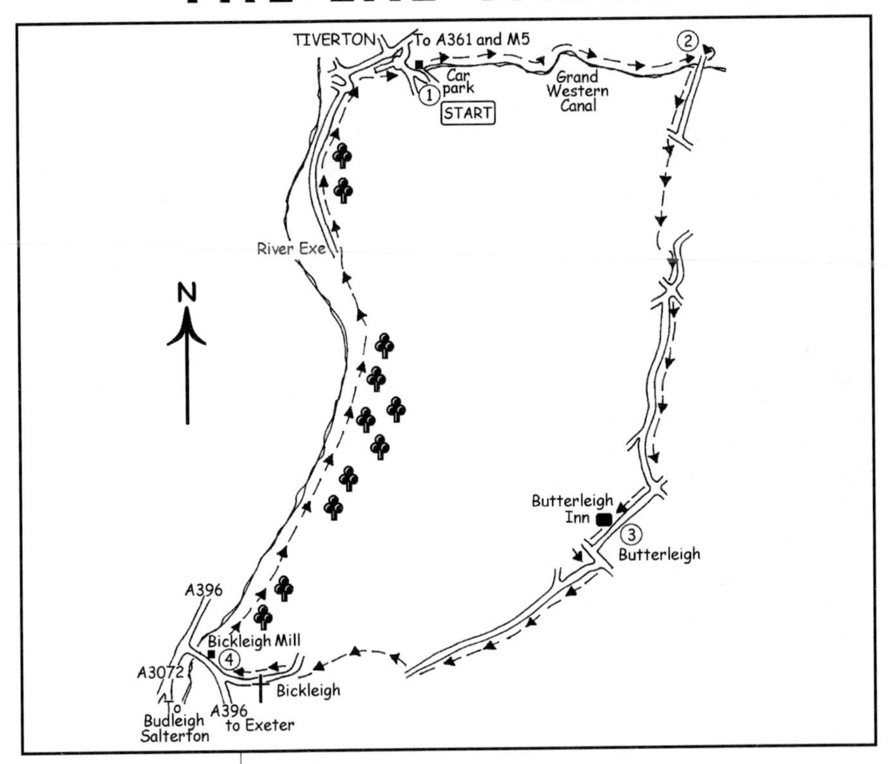

Distance: 10½ miles

Starting point: *The pay-and-display car park at the Grand Western Canal, Tiverton. GR 961124*

Maps: OS Explorer 114 Exeter and the Exe Valley; OS Landranger 181 Minehead and Brendon Hills (start and finish), 192 Exeter and Sidmouth (middle section)

How to get there: *Turn into Tiverton from the A361 North Devon Link Road or take the A396 from Exeter, and follow the signs for the Grand Western Canal.*

This walk comprises two delightful but very different waterside paths, linked by peaceful, flower-filled lanes and green lanes. It gives you the opportunity to explore this lovely but relatively unknown area of mid-Devon without too much effort. Do be sure to go suitably shod, however; the green lanes are rather wet and muddy in places – not a problem in itself, provided you are not wearing your best shoes!

The Butterleigh Inn, a 17th-century hostelry, is an absolute gem. The bar has a tiled floor and half-panelled walls, with pine tables and benches, while the separate lounge area is carpeted and furnished with chairs and settles, and has a wood-burning stove. Off the bar, there is a delightful little snug, and outside a patio beer garden. There are no fruit machines and no jukebox, just a very warm welcome and a number of real ales.

The food *is all home made, and ranges from soup and snacks to main courses. They always have a good range of vegetarian dishes available. Telephone: 01884 855407.*

① Go to the end of the car park and pass the tea garden at the end (a delightful place to refresh yourself if you want something before you start). This path takes you up to the canal towpath.

Today, the Grand Western Canal is a pretty though fairly insignificant waterway, but, as its name suggests, when it was first envisaged the planners dreamed of something much more ambitious. One aim was to provide a route from the Somerset coast to Exeter so that coal from Wales did not have to be brought all the way round Land's End. Another was to link Bristol with the English Channel, while the most ambitious of all envisaged linking it with other waterways to connect London and Exeter.

Alas, none of these plans came to fruition. The first stretch, 11 miles from Tiverton to the Somerset border, was completed in 1814, and twenty years later it was extended to Taunton; but that

BICKLEIGH MILL

is as far as it went, as it was superseded by other forms of transport. Indeed, even the new section only operated for a little over thirty years. The original canal continued to be used but fell into decline after the 1920s. It was revived in the 1960s, and is now designated as a country park.

You are greeted immediately by a beautiful scene, especially if you happen upon it in summer. There are water lilies and yellow iris along the banks, ducks, coots and swans (and, if you are lucky, their young) on the water, and dog roses hanging over the path. At first there are houses on the opposite bank, but after a while you will leave **Tiverton** behind and meet just the odd dog-walker or angler, or the occasional boat. There are now trees overhanging the canal. You pass under three bridges; when you have gone under the third, which is **Manley Bridge**, go left to leave the towpath. (1½ miles)

② Turn left at the lane on the bank above and cross the bridge over the canal. This is a pretty, peaceful lane, which leads to nowhere important and therefore carries little traffic.

The hedgerows alongside are full of flowers in summer. It climbs steadily away from the canal for about 700 yards to a junction. Go straight on along a green lane, which continues to climb between flower-filled hedges. At the top it levels off and becomes rather muddy. It then starts to descend between high banks and becomes wet rather than muddy. The trees form a green arch overhead.

At the bottom of the hill cross a log bridge and swing left to enter a wood and meet a lane. Turn right and follow the lane up a short hill to a crossroads; go straight across (signposted to **Butterleigh**). At the next junction go straight on. As you go you get a pleasant view across a patchwork of fields and hedges. You pass a farm on the left, and at the next junction go straight on again (signposted to **Butterleigh**, **Cullompton** and **Bradninch**). At the next crossroads, turn right (there is a sign pointing to Butterleigh, but it is virtually in the hedge). After about 500 yards you enter the delightful village of Butterleigh, and will find the **Butterleigh Inn** on your right. You are now over a third of the way along the walk, and probably deserve some refreshment. (2½ miles)

THE BUTTERLEIGH INN, BUTTERLEIGH

③ Carry on through the village, and at the T-junction turn left (signposted to **Bickleigh**). At the next junction go round to the right, and at the next straight on. You pass the drives for **Underleigh** and **Higher Brithayes** farms, and then a house called **Lower Brithayes**. Two hundred yards beyond **Lower Brithayes**, you will see a green lane going off to the right; follow it. Like the previous green lanes you have been following, it is filled with flowers and birdsong.

It climbs between high hedges and then levels off slightly, becoming rather muddy as it does so. After a long but fairly gentle climb of just over $^1/_2$ mile you emerge onto a lane. Bear left and follow the lane into **Bickleigh**, another very attractive village, passing the church as you go.

To say that Bampfylde Moore Carew was eccentric would be an understatement. Born at Bickleigh Castle, just across the River Exe, in the 18th century, he was a member of one of the foremost families in Devon (his father was Rector of Bickleigh) and was educated at Blundell's School in Tiverton, but nevertheless decided to make his living as a beggar. He ran away from school to join a band of gypsies and, having learned everything they could teach him, embarked on a career as a vagabond.

A master of disguise, he appeared all over South Devon, sometimes as a shipwrecked mariner, also as a one-legged miner, a poor widow and a clergyman who had resigned his living over a matter of conscience. In 1739 he was arrested and sold into slavery in America, but managed to escape, took refuge with some Indians and begged his passage home. Back in England he was something of a celebrity, and counted many of the aristocracy among his friends. After another spell in America, from which he escaped again, and six months in prison, he finally retired and returned to live in Bickleigh. He is buried at his father's church.

Follow the lane through the village to the main road. When you reach it, bear right along a side road, which takes you to **Bickleigh Mill**. ($2^1/_2$ miles)

Bickleigh Mill, a beautiful old water mill, is now a series of shops, including a craft shop and a farm shop. There is also a working pottery and a lovely tea garden by the river (telephone 01884 855419 for more information).

If you want to visit **Bickleigh Castle**, you need to make a detour of about $1^1/_2$ miles across the river. Continue past **Bickleigh Mill** to the main road again, cross the bridge and turn left onto the A3072, then left again down a lane.

④ Just before the stone bridge at **Bickleigh Mill**, turn right and go through a gate marked with the **Exe Valley Way** waymark. This path passes to the right of the mill and goes through another two gates. It runs alongside the old mill leat and through yet another gate into a wood. At the junction go straight on. The path becomes a track and follows the leat to the point where the latter leaves the **River Exe**. Here it veers to the right slightly; this stretch can become muddy after rain.

The track narrows to a path again and runs down to rejoin the river. This is a lovely stretch; the ground is carpeted with pink purslane in summer as well as buttercups and cow parsley, the wood stretches up to the right and the river flows sedately along on your left. You eventually leave the wood via a stile. Keep to the left of the field beyond, alongside the river. At the end you will find a gate and stile on your right; cross over. (At the time of writing the gate is wired closed and the stile broken, so one has to climb over the gate, but hopefully the stile will soon be repaired.)

Turn left on the other side and continue alongside the river. Cross a small footbridge and then a stile to enter another wood. After a while you cross another stile in a fence on the right and go up across an open stretch into another piece of woodland. Cross yet another stile. As you walk through this wood you get further and further from the river. You eventually go through a gate, cross a track and go through another gate back into the wood. Where the track turns right up the hill, turn left, following the **Exe Valley Way** waymark. Cross another stile and go along the bottom of the field beyond; towards the end you will find a gap in the hedge on the left; go through and turn right.

You pass a sewage works, cross a stile and follow a path among some trees and across another stile onto a concrete drive. Go straight on. This drive joins a lane, which rejoins the river and runs through a wood to **Tiverton**. At the T-junction on the outskirts of the town, turn right and follow a residential road to a roundabout. Turn right onto the pavement alongside the main road. Soon the pavement ends and a path goes up to the right, above the road. Follow it to another road and go straight on to a small roundabout. Turn right here up **Canal Hill**, and you will find the car park on the left after about 300 yards. (4 miles)

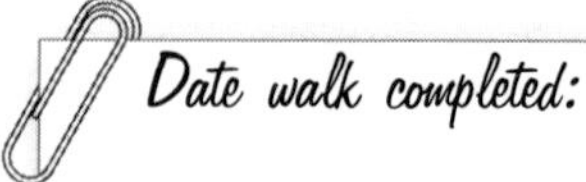

Walk 8

MISTS, MYTHS AND MYSTERIES: BELSTONE COMMON AND SKAIGH WOOD

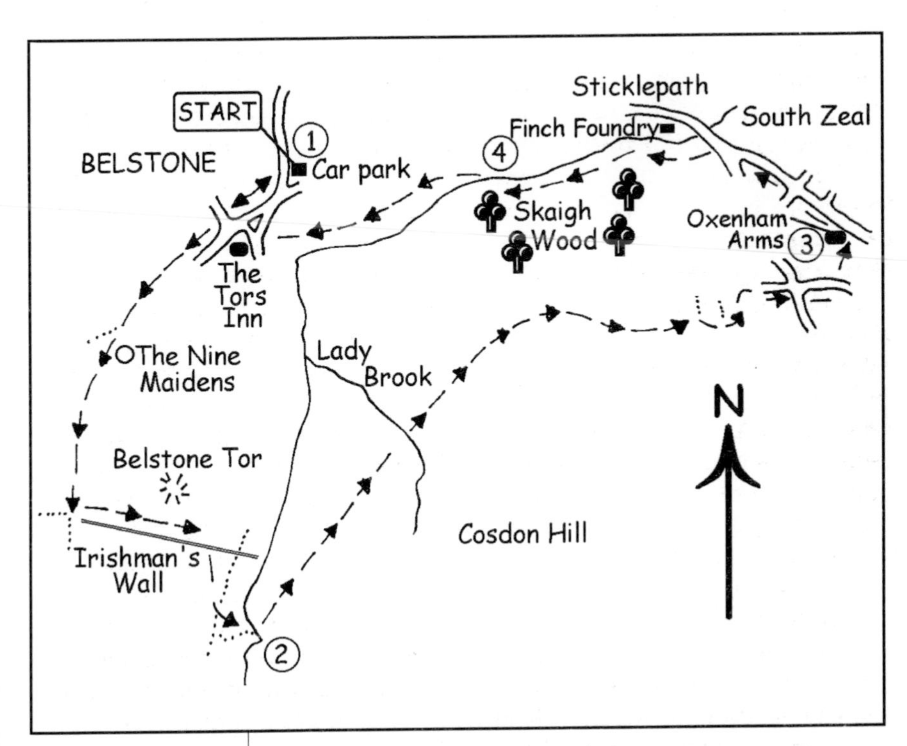

Distance:
7½ miles

Starting point:
The car park on the left as you enter the village of Belstone. GR 621938

Maps: OS Explorer OL28 Dartmoor or 113 Okehampton; OS Landranger 191 Okehampton and North Dartmoor

How to get there: *Belstone is just south of the A30 near Okehampton, and clearly signposted from that road.*

The Oxenham Arms, in South Zeal, halfway round the walk, is a solid granite building. It was built by lay monks in the 12th century (the 'Zeal' in the village's name refers to a monk's cell).

As one would expect in a building of this era, there are thick walls, beamed ceilings and leaded windows, and the cosy bar has a massive granite fireplace. In addition to this bar there is a small family lounge with a 5,000-year-old monolith built into one of the walls. Across a passage is a delightful dining room, and there is a large garden at the back. It is a charming pub, oozing atmosphere.

The food *is imaginative and delicious and ranges from soups and sandwiches to specials such as Chicken Cacciatore and their renowned steak, kidney, Guinness and mushroom pie. Telephone: 01837 840244.*

The Walk

① Turn left as you leave the car park and follow the lane into **Belstone**. It is a most attractive village of granite and cob cottages. Go right the way through, ignoring the turnings to left and right, and climb the hill out of the village on the other side. Go through a gate at the end of the lane onto the open moor.

Follow the track on the other side as it runs alongside a wall. The views start immediately, to the right across a patchwork of fields and to the left over the rolling moorland. Then, as you come to the top of a rise, an equally stunning vista opens up ahead to **Yes Tor** and **High**

The north-east corner of Dartmoor is a land of mists and legends, but see it on a sunny day and its beauty will take your breath away. This route shows this area at its very best, and in two very different guises: the rolling moor itself and the beautiful wooded valleys of what is called the 'in country' – the gentler landscapes on the periphery. The views from the open moorland are breathtaking, and the woodland below is quite magical. There is also a lot to interest the passer by, from sites full of mystery and strange tales to delightful villages. Be prepared for a steep climb near the start and one or two less strenuous ones later on, and go suitably shod to cross a shallow ford.

THE NINE MAIDENS

Willhays, the highest point on Dartmoor. Soon the wall swings round to the right; there is a wide grassy path that follows it round but you need to keep to the main track, which goes straight on. After about 150 yards there is a fork; take the left-hand track. After another 150 yards or so look to the left and you will see the **Nine Maidens** (marked as the **Nine Stones** on the Ordnance Survey maps) about 75 yards from the track.

Legend has it that these stones are the remains of young girls who were turned to stone for dancing on the Sabbath. But why* Nine *Maidens, when there are not nine stones but seventeen? And why were these particular girls punished in this way when they could hardly have been the only ones to indulge in frivolity on a Sunday? The answer could lie in the fact that nine was regarded as a magical number in ancient times, and the circle was believed to have been used in witchcraft and moon worship. So the reference to the Sabbath is probably a corruption of 'sabbat', the witches' ritual. Rather boringly, the word 'maiden' is almost certainly a corruption of the Celtic word* maen, *meaning simply 'stone'. The circle is in fact the remains of an ancient burial cairn.

Continue along the track. It becomes rather rough and rocky for a while and then, a little over ½ mile after the fork, you will see a much clearer track coming in from the right to join yours. This point is where **Irishman's Wall** begins; it runs up the hill to the left. It is not very obviously a wall here, but as you look up the hill you can see its path – initially no more than a line of rocks – becoming clearer higher up. Turn left off the track and follow the wall up the hill.

Under ancient tradition, local farmers had the right to enclose up to 8 acres of moorland for their own use. Towards the beginning of the 19th century, however, two farmers hired a group of Irishmen to enclose a much greater area on Belstone Common. They had built about a mile of wall when the other local farmers realised what was happening. The resulting enclosure would have restricted their access to the moor quite considerably, so they gathered at the wall and, at a given signal, pushed it over. The Irishmen departed, never to be seen again, but parts of their wall remain – even if its name does appear to give credit for the enterprise to just one Irishman.

It is a steep climb, and halfway up there is a large patch of loose rocks, known as **clitter**. It is probably easiest to circle round it to avoid a lot of scrambling, but if you are feeling particularly adventurous (and fit), you may prefer to clamber across it (it is not particularly difficult).

Beyond the clitter the wall becomes considerably more distinct, and as you get to the top it is quite clearly a wall. As you climb you get a lovely view to the left down the valley of the **East Okement** and across the farms of mid-Devon. Stop when you get to the top, not just to catch your breath but also to appreciate the stunning panorama that now unfolds before you. Every time I climb up here I find myself gasping at the scale and beauty of what I can see – it is like being on top of the world. To the north lie the fields and woods of mid-Devon, stretching to Exmoor on the horizon, and to the south, east and west the apparently endless rolling wastes of Dartmoor, with the clouds making patterns of light and shade on the landscape as they scud across the wide sky. If you are planning on a picnic or coffee break, this is the place to have it, so that you have time to absorb the atmosphere and sense of space.

Irishman's Wall goes steeply down the other side of the hill, and if the visibility is not too good you might want to follow it until you reach a track, at which point you turn right. However, there is a quicker and easier route down. You should be able to see the **River Taw** below you, with a bend in it about 300 yards to the right of Irishman's Wall. It is at that bend that you need to cross it, so you can make your way more gently down the hill in that direction. On this slope you will find whortleberry plants interspersed with the yellow of gorse and tormentil and the purple of heather in late summer. Cross the track at the bottom and make your way down to a ford in the bend of the river (if you have followed the wall and track, you will find another track going left to the ford $\frac{1}{4}$ mile from the bottom of the wall). ($2\frac{1}{2}$ miles)

② On the other side of the river, as the track goes right, climb the bank ahead and go half-left. There is no path, but you should make your way gradually up the hill. At the far left-hand end of the ridge you will see a rock and a tree on the horizon; aim for a point about 100 yards to the right of them. You do not have to be too precise about your direction, as you can always correct for any error when you reach the top.

As you come over the ridge the views open up again, across the farms to Exmoor on the left and over the moorland behind you. There is a shallow valley to your right, with **Cosdon Hill** on the other side. Your route will take you gently down at an angle, into the valley. At some point you should meet a sunken path coming in from the right alongside a stream. Follow it down to cross the stream and then again on the other side as it skirts round **Cosdon Hill**. The path is quite clear, and follows a dried-up leat.

About $\frac{1}{2}$ mile after crossing the stream you will cross a track leading up the hill on your right. Carry on round the hill and another track will cross yours; turn left onto it and then right along it. It leads you down off the moor and between two walls. About $\frac{1}{2}$ mile after joining it you come to a gate with a T-junction just beyond. Turn right (signposted to the **A30** and **South Zeal**). At the next junction go right again (again signposted to the **A30** and **South Zeal**). At the next, turn left and after a few yards right down a path between banks. This path is simply a short cut to cut off a bend in the track, saving about 50 yards. It emerges where the track becomes a surfaced lane.

Turn right and follow the lane to a road; cross over and follow the lane on the other side down into **South Zeal**. Just before you reach a house called **Moorlands** on your right turn left through a gate. There is no

THE OXENHAM ARMS, SOUTH ZEAL

signpost, but it is a right of way. Cross the field on the other side to the corner of a hedge alongside the village playing field. Follow the path along the left of the hedge and leave the field via a kissing gate. This leads into a lane; follow it round to the right to the main street. Turn left and you will find a delightful old pub, the **Oxenham Arms**, on the left after a few yards. You are two-thirds of the way through the walk and deserve a break – and I can think of few better places to have one. (2½ miles)

③ Continue along the main street through the pretty village, passing a little chapel on the left. At the crossroads at the end of the village go straight on (signposted to **Sticklepath**). When you reach the edge of **Sticklepath** you will come to a T-junction; cross over the main road to a track beside the **River Taw** (signposted to the **moor**, **Skaigh Wood** and **Skaigh**). At the end of the track is a gate; go through and turn right to follow the river. You cross a stile to enter **Skaigh Wood**. You eventually come to a gate leading onto a footbridge carved with a quotation from the book, *Tarka the Otter*. (1½ miles)

④ On the other side of the bridge follow the path round to the right. At the T-junction turn left (signposted to **Belstone** and the **moor**). The river is now about 20 yards down on your left. After 300 yards or so you will see a path leading left down to another footbridge; ignore it and carry straight on. The path eventually leaves the wood and winds and climbs up the bracken-covered hillside. It is a steep but mercifully short climb.

At the junction near the top go left to join a wall. You now get a good view up the valley of the Taw to the moor. The path emerges onto a large grassy area on the outskirts of **Belstone.** Climb to a track and bear right just beyond it to a junction of three lanes. Bear right between the buildings. If you are ready for some refreshment, you will find the **Tors Inn** on your left.

At the T-junction just beyond the pub turn right and follow the lane out of the village. At the junction on the edge, follow the main lane round to the left to the car park. (1 mile)

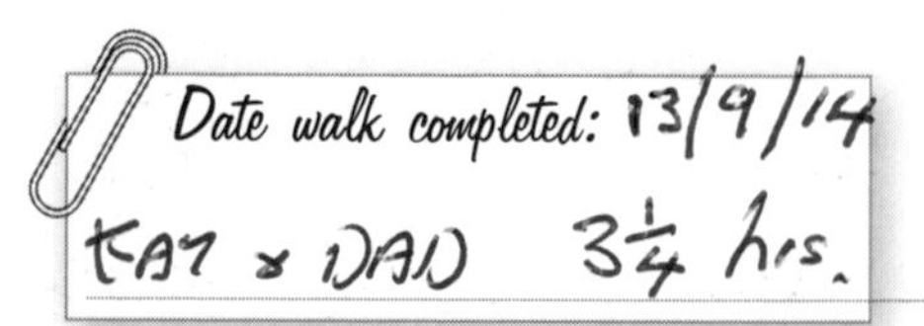

Walk 9

WOODS AND WATER: THE TEIGN GORGE

PART OF THE RAMPARTS, CRANBROOK CASTLE

Distance:
11½ miles

Starting point:
The car park just west of Steps Bridge. GR 803883

Maps: OS Explorer OL28 Dartmoor; OS Landranger 191 Okehampton and North Dartmoor

How to get there: *Steps Bridge is on the B3212 between Exeter and Moretonhampstead and just west of Dunsford.*

The Fingle Bridge Inn, halfway round the route, was built in 1897. It is an attractive hostelry overlooking the River Teign at one of its most beautiful points. It has a spacious bar with a beamed ceiling and two granite fireplaces, one containing a wood-burning stove. It is decorated with old angling equipment and fishing prints (a tribute to the river's popularity with anglers). There is also a large, airy restaurant. The place to be in summer, however, is outside on the terraces, watching the river flow by. Attached to the pub is a shop selling ice-creams.

The food *is all home made, and ranges from delicious and filling soups to sandwiches and baguettes and a mouthwatering array of fish and meat dishes. Devon cream teas are also available. Telephone: 01647 281287.*

① Cross the road to a concrete track, which is signposted to a youth hostel and is also indicated as a bridle- and footpath. When it curves to the left, follow it round rather than following the unsurfaced track that goes straight on. Then, when you come to some steps up to the youth hostel after a few yards, bear right up a path (signposted to **Heltor Farm** and the road near **Westcott**). It climbs through the lovely **Bridford Wood**, with a mass of bilberries (known locally as whortleberries) alongside. Then, as you get higher, the whortleberries become interspersed with heather. You will find yourself walking along a ridge, with steep-sided valleys on either side, and occasionally you will

The Teign gorge must rate as one of the loveliest areas in Devon. Heavily wooded and sheltered by the steep slopes on either side, it is an idyllic spot to wander through. And if you are prepared to climb out of the valley the views will take your breath away. This walk gives you the best of both worlds: it starts with a walk through Bridford Wood, then follows lanes, paths and green lanes to Mardon Down, where you can enjoy superb vistas in all directions. You then return to the gorge via an Iron Age hillfort, and the final leg is a delightful stroll through the woods along the riverbank. There is a fair amount of climbing, especially towards the beginning of the walk, but there is so much to see along the way that one hardly notices it!

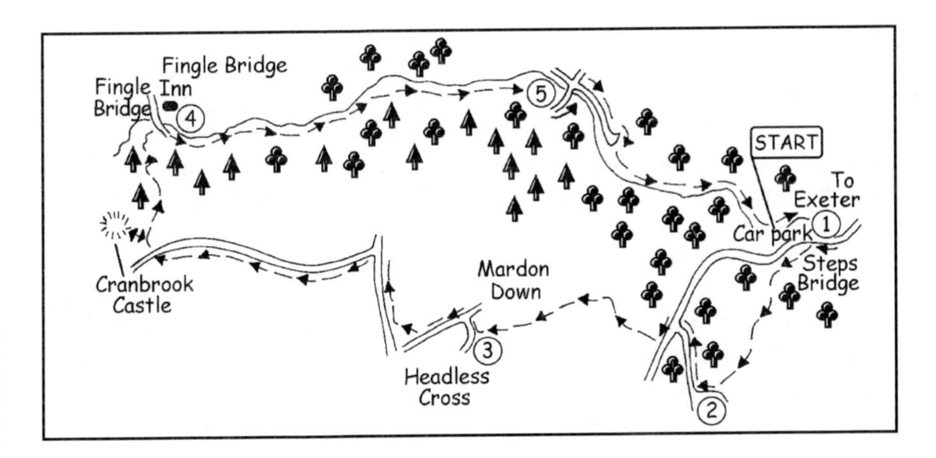

be able to see across the valleys through the trees.

After about 500 yards or so, you will come to a fork: go left and follow the path as it swings left to leave the wood via a ladder stile. Cross the field on the other side, following the yellow waymarks, to a gate. Keep to the left of the next field; look back as you go for a lovely view across the **Teign gorge** to the patchwork of fields beyond. Go through another gate and along the left-hand side of another field, then through yet another gate onto a green lane.

This brings you to a farm; turn left just before you reach it and follow a track round to the right past some cottages. Go through a gateway to a track. Cross it and bear left to a path alongside a wall. This leads up to a gate. Keep right across the field beyond. Look back for another superb view across the woods and fields. Just before you get to the end of the field, you will see a path through the gorse on the right; follow it for a few yards to a stile, and then for a few yards more to another stile, which takes you onto a lane. ($1\frac{1}{4}$ miles)

② Turn right and follow the lane as it winds steeply downhill to a T-junction; turn right again. You re-enter a wood and continue to descend, though rather less steeply. After 700 yards or so of lovely woodland walking you emerge at the B3212. Turn left, and after 200 yards, just by the 'Sharp bends' road sign, you will find a gate on the right. There is a public bridlepath sign, but it is not very clear as it is hidden behind the gate. Keep to the right of a field to another gate. Cross a stream and keep to the left of the next field to another gate, which leads into a green lane.

Follow this round to the left and

to the right. When it swings left again towards a gate, go through another gate on the right, following the path sign. This path climbs steeply through bracken and brambles to a wood. It passes through a gate on the left and then goes right to continue climbing. After a few yards you go through another gate and after a few more yards you come to a track; turn right and continue to climb. As you do so, console yourself that all this climbing will result in views that will amaze you. When you come to some farm buildings, turn left up a green lane to a gate. Follow the green lane on the other side. Like most green lanes, this is a haven for birds and wild flowers. Particularly attractive in late summer and early autumn are the rowan berries that abound in the hedges on either side.

After 1/4 mile you go through another gate and out onto **Mardon Down**. As you do so, look to your right and behind you for a stunning panorama of woods and fields. Follow the broad grassy track that leads straight on from the gate. It climbs gently and as it does so the view to the right and behind you gets even better. When you get to the top of the small rise another breathtaking vista opens up across the open moor ahead and to the right. (2 miles)

③ The track comes out at a small parking area, beyond which is a lane. On the other side of the lane you will see the **Headless Cross**.

Also called the Maximajor Stone, the Headless Cross is not in fact the remains of a cross, despite its name. The original stone was more likely a prehistoric standing stone, but sadly what you can see is not the original. That was destroyed by vandals in 1990 and has been replaced by a replica.

Turn right along the lane and at the T-junction 150 yards further on turn left. After another 1/4 mile, as the lane curves to the left you will see a track on the right; turn along it. This part of **Mardon Down** is full of rowan trees, and the berries provide a lovely splash of red to go with the yellow of the gorse in late summer.

The track comes out at another lane; turn right and after a few yards cross a cattle grid. Continue along the lane for another 600 yards to a junction; turn left (signposted to **Chagford**). Like the ones that have preceded it, this is another quiet, virtually traffic-free lane, lined with hedges and wild flowers. At the next junction, follow the main lane round to the right. There is more climbing, I'm afraid, but not for too long, and at the top you get another lovely view over the moor to the left, with the distinctive shape of **Haytor** on the horizon.

The lane goes to the right; look out for deer in the field on the right as it does so. Shortly after the bend, you will see the great bulk of **Williamstone Rock** on your right. The lane climbs some more; at the next junction go straight on (signposted to **Chagford**). The lane descends again, passes a farm and then – you guessed it – climbs again. It is not a very steep ascent this time, however, and you can spur yourself on with the thought that, apart from a short stretch up to **Cranbrook Castle** if you decide to visit it, this is the last climb of the walk!

About 300 yards after passing the farm the lane curves to the left; as it does so you will see a track leading off to the right (there is a sign pointing to **Fingle Bridge** and **Cranbrook Castle**, but since it is a little way down the track, it is not much help). Turn along here. After 100 yards you will find a gate on your left, with a sign hidden in the undergrowth pointing to **Cranbrook Castle**. It is worth the 200-yard detour to the ramparts of this Iron Age hillfort, if only for the views.

The woods below you once formed part of the estate of Castle Drogo, a stately home now owned by the National Trust, which was designed by Sir Edwin Lutyens and built between 1911 and 1930 for Julius Drew, the founder of the Home and Colonial Stores. Despite its name, it is, in fact, a country house rather than a castle, but the estate is extensive, and the views from the house itself, which sits on a promontory above the Teign Gorge, are quite stunning. If you want to visit the house, there are paths leading up to it from Fingle Bridge.

To continue the walk, carry on down the track. At the junction go left along the main track (signposted to **Fingle Bridge**). It winds through the lovely **Charles Wood**, descending all the time. As you get near the bottom you will begin to hear the **River Teign** gurgling along below you, and then you will see it. You reach the river at **Fingle Bridge**, with a car park on your right. Cross the 16th-century bridge to quench your thirst at the delightful **Fingle Bridge Inn**. (3½ miles)

④ To continue the walk, cross back over the bridge and go through the car park, following the sign for **Clifford Bridge**. Follow the clear path on the other side, a little way away from the river. After a while it goes through an old gateway on the right and past some ruined buildings, then bears left. You soon join the river and go through a gate, continuing on the broad track along the bank. For the next 2½ miles you will be walking through the most delightful wood, usually with the river tumbling and gliding alongside you.

When you come to a fork, about ¼ mile after going through the gate, take the left-hand track, alongside the river. The broadleaved woodland gives way to conifers and you veer slightly away from the river, although you can still hear it over on your left. After a clear stretch, the broadleaves start again and you rejoin the river. You finally leave the river and the wood via a stile onto a lane. (2½ miles)

⑤ Turn left and cross the river, then follow the lane round to the right. After 200 yards or so you will come to a crossroads; turn right (signposted with a footpath sign to **Steps Bridge** and with a road sign to **Dunsford**). This lane runs parallel with the river but a short distance away. Then, 600 yards after the crossroads, it swings left. Just after it does so, turn right through a gate (signposted to **Steps Bridge**), cross a footbridge and bear right to enter **Dunsford Wood**.

Dunsford and Meadhaydown woods, which stretch all the way to Steps Bridge, are both nature reserves, and there is a wealth of bird life to be seen among the trees and on the river, including wagtails, kingfishers, herons, woodpeckers and dippers. The area is also renowned for its wild flowers, starting with snowdrops in February, followed by daffodils, wood anemones and wild garlic, with foxgloves predominating in the summer. There are otters in the river.

The path runs alongside the river for much of its length, although from time to time you will find yourself directed away from it in order to prevent erosion of the old riverside route. It is quite beautiful, with the sunlight filtering through the trees and dappling the water, and the wood stretching up the steep slope on your left. You finally leave **Meadhaydown Wood** via a gap in the wall, and turn right on the road beyond. Cross **Steps Bridge** and follow the road round to the right. There is a tea room offering refreshments and light lunches just before you reach the car park. (2¼ miles)

Date walk completed:

FAITHLESS WIVES AND FICKLE MAIDENS: THE SOUTH AND NORTH TEIGN RIVERS

NORTH CREABER FARM

Distance:
$11^3/_4$ miles

Starting point:
The public car park at Fernworthy reservoir. GR 669838

Maps: OS Explorer OL28 Dartmoor; OS Landranger 191 Okehampton and North Dartmoor

How to get there: *Turn north-west off the B3212 Moretonhampstead to Princetown road, following the signs for Fernworthy reservoir, or take the B3206 west from the A382 Moretonhampstead to Okehampton road to Chagford and follow the signs from there.*

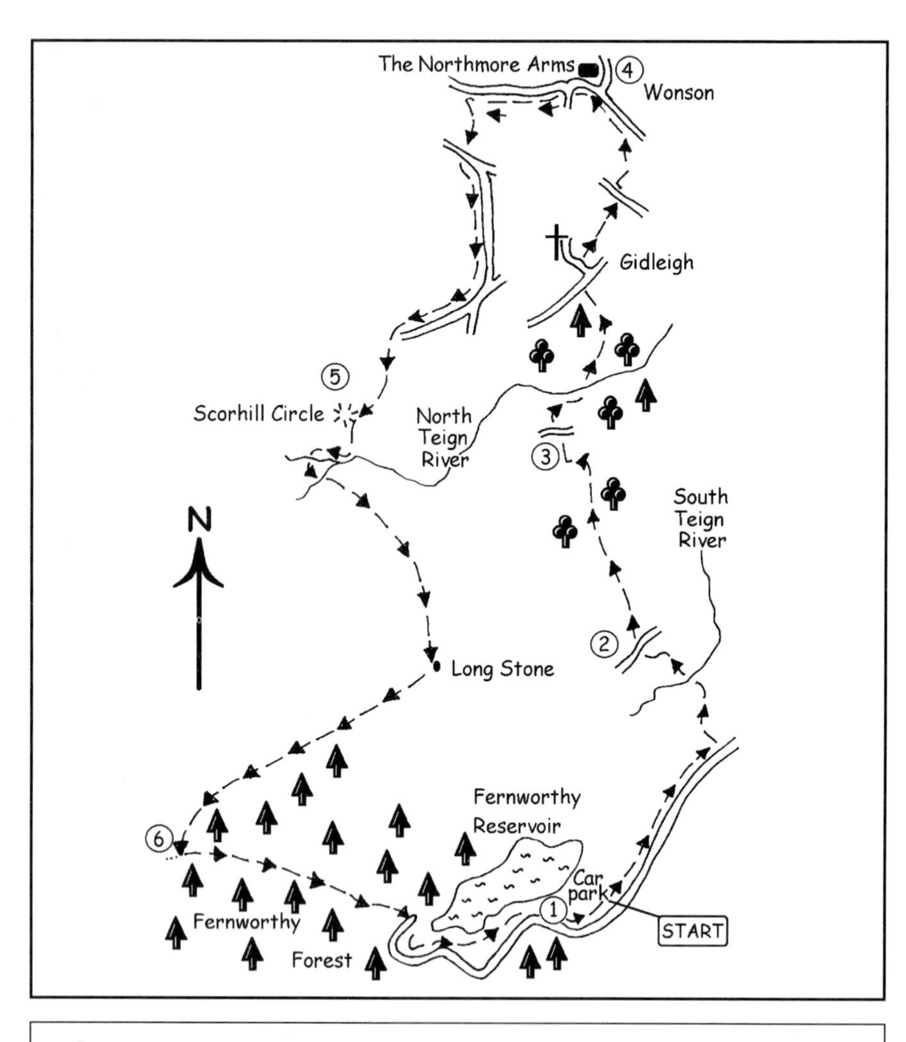

Green lanes, farm paths and forest tracks, conifer plantations, deciduous woods and open moorland – these are the main features of this beautiful and relatively undemanding route. There are also extensive views and a pretty little village, plus a bit of history and a rather politically incorrect folk story. There are one or two steep climbs, but they are short and should not trouble most walkers unduly.

The Northmore Arms in Wonson, halfway round the route, is a lovely little pub which just oozes atmosphere. Some 400 years old, it comprises two small, interlinked rooms, both with massive, bare granite walls and small windows. The main bar has a large fireplace with an open fire, while the other room is heated by a wood-burning stove. Across the drive is an attractive little beer garden. It lies on the Mariners' Way, and is said to be haunted by a sailor (some say a pirate) who stopped off here and never made it to his ship.

It is very much a local pub, and usually has three traditional beers on offer (for some time now these have been Cotleigh Tawney, Dob's and Adnam's Broadside).

It is open *all day, offering a range of good, home-made staples, including both snacks and main courses. Telephone: 01647 231428.*

① Leave the car park and turn left to follow the road back across a cattle grid and out of the forest onto the open moor. As you go, you can see the outline of **Kestor** half-left on the horizon; you will be seeing this rock from various angles later in the walk. Half-right, you can see the rocky outcrop on the top of **Meldon Hill**. The road descends to a cattle grid and 50 yards beyond it you will come to a track on the left, signposted as the **Mariners' Way** and the **Two Moors Way** to **Teigncombe** and **Gidleigh**. Turn off the road here.

The Mariners' Way is an ancient route from North to South Devon, which was used by sailors who had been signed off at one end of the county and were making their way to join new ships at the other.

Follow the track to a farm and go to the left and then to the right past the house. Go through a gate into a field and keep to the right. At the end you will come to two gates; take the left-hand one and keep to the right of the next field to a stile. Make your way down the hill on the other side to the **South Teign River** and when you get there turn left and follow the river upstream for a short distance to a footbridge. Cross it and keep to the left of the field beyond, climbing steeply up a hill – fortunately a fairly short one. When you get to the top, pause to look back for a good view across the valley.

At the top of the field you join a track; go through a gate at the end and left along a broad path (do not go through any of the gates on either side). After a short distance you come to a drive; cross it and bear left, following the path sign. The path swings to the right and passes through a gate onto a track by some farm buildings. After a few yards you emerge onto a lane. (1¾ miles)

② Turn right and then immediately left along a broad track (signposted to **Gidleigh**). When you come to a gate, bear right along a path, which takes you through a small wooded area to a gate. Keep to the left of the field on the other side; as you go you get an attractive view over to the right to **Meldon Hill**. Cross a stile at the end and continue along the path to the left of a stretch of waste ground, which is full of the delicately flowered Himalayan balsam in late summer. The path goes to the left to another stile into a field.

Go right and along the side of the field to yet another stile, which leads onto a track. Cross that to a fourth stile, following the **Mariners' Way** sign, and cross the field beyond to another stile (the fifth in succession if you are still counting). There is a boardwalk to follow along the next stretch because the ground underfoot can become boggy; this area is full of an interesting variety of marsh plants as well as the ubiquitous gorse.

The path takes you through a gate and across the next field to yet another stile; bear right to cross a track and follow the path sign on the other side. This takes you past a wooded area with a small rill on your left. You then cross the rill and a stile and follow another boardwalk. Cross a field to a footbridge followed by a stile; bear right to cross the rill again and then left alongside it, along the edge of a field. At the end go through a gate on the left and then, after a few yards, through another gate. Cross a track to a green lane signposted to **Kestor** and **Gidleigh**. (¾ mile)

③ This green lane climbs between walls and trees; at the junction, turn right along a broad track (signposted to **Gidleigh**). This takes you to a lane; turn left and almost immediately right. Cross a stile and follow the path down a hill; at the bottom turn right to enter **Gidleigh Wood** and then after a short distance left to go down through the wood to the **North Teign River**. Cross the river via a footbridge. There are deer here and you may be lucky enough to glimpse one, but they are usually well hidden among the trees. It is an idyllic spot, with the dense wood around you and the river cascading over the rocks alongside.

Follow the path away from the river and right along a track. After a short distance you will see a path sign pointing left off the track into a conifer plantation. A steep but short climb follows through the densely planted trees. At the top the trees thin out somewhat, allowing for some undergrowth. You go through a clearing, with a lovely view across the fields, hedges and woods ahead of you, to a broad track. Follow it alongside the plantation to a gate and a lane; turn right and after 150 yards left (signposted to **Gidleigh** and **Chapple**). You pass **Way Cottage** on your left; you can carry on for a few yards to see **Gidleigh Church** and **Castle**, or turn right down a green lane to continue the walk.

Follow the green lane (there is a sign to **Gidleigh Mill**, but it is a long way down, so you will not see it from the main lane). It runs for about 1/4 mile to a surfaced drive; carry straight on down to a lane. Turn left and then, after 150 yards, right to cross a stream and follow another surfaced drive (signposted to **Providence Place**). At the end, go through a gate and bear right to follow a green lane on the other side. It climbs steadily, with occasional glimpses of the open moor through gateways on the left. You come out at a lane; turn left, and at the junction 1/4 mile further on turn right (signposted to **Wonson** and **Throwleigh**). After a few yards you come to the little hamlet of **Wonson**, with the welcome sight of the **Northmore Arms** on the left. (2 1/4 miles)

④ When you leave the pub, turn right and go back to the junction; turn right (signposted to **Forder**, **Chapple** and **Gidleigh**). At the next junction, turn right (signposted to **Ash**). After 700 yards or so you cross a cattle grid; on the other side you will find a signpost pointing left for the **Mariners' Way to Moortown**. Turn off the road and follow the direction of the sign through the gorse. You cross a small clapper bridge and turn left to follow the path through the gorse and trees to a track. Go straight on and the track will emerge onto a road; turn left.

After 200 yards you come to a junction; follow the main lane round to the right (signposted to **Creaber**, **Scorhill** and **Gidleigh**). At the next junction go straight on (signposted to **Creaber** and **Scorhill**). After another 200 yards you come to yet another junction; turn right (signposted to **Creaber**). This lane climbs and winds up to the moor. At the end, go through a gate and follow the left-hand track on the other side. When it peters out, follow the boundary wall on your left. When it bends to the left follow it round, looking out to your right for a superb panorama across the moor – not a house, not a road, not a tree to be seen, just miles of contoured moorland and an infinity of sky. To your left you can see the other face of this part of Devon – the woods and farms rolling away into the distance.

When the wall bends to the left again, go straight on; there is no clear path, but after 100 yards you will come to a grassy track. Turn right along it; as you go, you continue to enjoy the view across the moor, with (from left to right) **Watern Tor**, **Wild Tor** and **Steeperton Tor** on the horizon. After 200 yards you come to a fork; go right to reach **Scorhill** (pronounced 'Scorrell') **Circle**. (2 miles)

Scorhill Circle is one of the finest and most evocative of Dartmoor's stone circles. It was erected about 4,500 years ago, but no one is quite sure exactly what purpose it served.

⑤ If you go straight down to the river from **Scorhill Circle** you will find the **Tolmen**, an enormous rock with a hole right through it, in the river immediately opposite the end of the belt of trees. This is another lovely spot for a picnic break, and to contemplate the fate of the women of Chagford.

The story is told of 'faithless wives and fickle maidens' from the ancient stannary town of Chagford being chased up to Gidleigh Common as a penance for their sins. They were made to run round Scorhill Circle three times before being sent down to the river and made to go through the hole in the Tolmen into the water below. They were then chased up to the Grey Wethers stone circles on the slopes of Sittaford Tor, beyond what is now Fernworthy Forest to the south, where each woman was made to kneel in front of a stone and pray for forgiveness. If she was forgiven, she was spared, but if not, the stone would fall down and crush her.

Follow the river upstream to a clapper bridge across a tributary, the **Walla Brook**, and then cross another clapper bridge across the **North Teign** a few yards beyond it. Follow the path up alongside the trees on the left; when you come to the end of the wall bear right along a grassy track, keeping **Kestor** on your left. You will see the remains of a cairn and a stone row on your right; when you reach the stone row, bear left to follow it. The stones are somewhat intermittent, but the path is quite clear. At the top of the rise you will come to the **Long Stone**.

This prehistoric standing stone almost certainly had some ritual significance for our forebears, but precisely what its purpose was is uncertain. It is, however, an impressive monolith, and was pressed into service in medieval times as a boundary marker. You

can see the initials GP (for Gidleigh Parish) and DC (for Duke of Cornwall) on two of the faces, indicating the ownership of the relevant areas.

Bear right from the Long Stone towards the far right-hand corner of **Fernworthy Forest**, which comes into view as you breast the rise. Again, there is no clear path but you can easily make your way across the moor, and as long as you keep aiming for that corner you will be fine. When you get to it, follow it round and keep alongside the forest boundary. You will come to a wall after 300 yards; cross a ladder stile and continue alongside the forest edge. You continue to enjoy the view across the moorland hills on your right. After almost 3/4 mile you come to another wall and cross another ladder stile. The forest boundary takes a bend to the left; follow it round and after 300 yards you will find a gate on the left. (2 3/4 miles)

⑥ Go through and follow the track through the trees on the other side. At the crossroads go straight on. The track begins to descend and soon another good view opens up ahead of you. You come to several junctions, but you should just continue straight on along the track you are on. About 1 1/4 miles after you entered the forest the track ends at a gate; go through onto a surfaced road and turn right.

After about 300 yards the road turns sharp left, and then after another 500 yards or so it turns sharp right. As it does so, turn left, following the direction indicated by a green- and red-waymarked post, to a gate. On the other side you will see a hide on your left from which you can watch the birds on **Fernworthy Reservoir**. The path bears right, still indicated by a red and green post. You now have the reservoir on your left. The path swings left to cross a footbridge; bear right on the other side. You will come to a junction; go straight on (signposted to the car park walks). The path finally comes out at a track; turn right and about 10 yards before the gate at the end of the track turn left, again following the red and green waymarks, to the car park. (2 1/4 miles)

Date walk completed:

Walk 11

EAST DEVON'S PEBBLEBED HEATH: WOODBURY AND EAST BUDLEIGH COMMONS

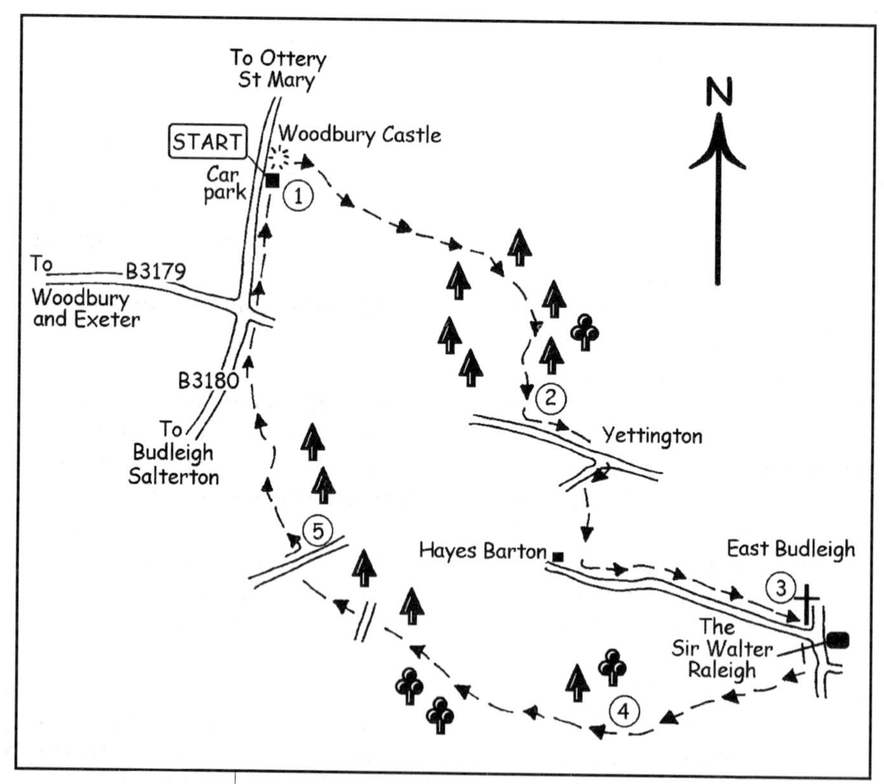

Distance:
$7^1/_4$ miles

Starting point:
The Woodbury Castle car park. GR 032872

Maps: OS Explorer 110 Exmouth and Sidmouth; OS Landranger 192 Exeter and Sidmouth

How to get there: *Woodbury Castle is on the B3180 Ottery St Mary to Budleigh Salterton road, about $^1/_2$ mile north of its junction with the B3179.*

The Sir Walter Raleigh in East Budleigh, halfway round the walk, is a 16th-century inn. It is certainly a delightful hostelry at which to break your journey. There is a small bar, with the low beams and small windows one associates with the period, although it is now furnished with padded benches and chairs. There is also a light, airy non-smoking restaurant and a beer garden.

The pub *prides itself on its hand-pumped beers, and there is always a selection on offer. The food, too, is excellent, and ranges from soup and pâté to a variety of main courses, with fish a speciality. Telephone: 01395 442510.*

The Walk

The B3180 runs through Woodbury Castle, an Iron Age hillfort, but the bulk of the site is to the east of the road. Built about 500 BC, it comprises an enormous rampart with a 20ft ditch outside it, and on the western side the defences are doubled, with a large fighting platform by the northern entrance. It is in a superb defensive position, with an excellent view over the Exe estuary. Indeed, its command of the local area is such that it was fortified and occupied as recently as 1798 as a defence against a possible invasion by Napoleon.

① When you have explored **Woodbury Castle**, go east (right if you are facing away from the car park) and then turn half-right to leave through a gap in the ramparts, following a clear path across the ditch. You come out at a track; turn left and then after a few yards right along another track. You get a

This is a very varied walk, taking you across the wide open spaces of Woodbury Common, with excellent views across to the coast, and through the lovely woods and lanes of East Budleigh. There is a great deal of interest to see along the way, including an Iron Age hillfort and the birthplace of Sir Walter Raleigh, not to mention the fascinating landscapes, flora and fauna of this very special area. Easy tracks take you across the common, while the return journey is mainly along green lanes. The latter tend to be rather muddy, however, so do dress accordingly.

superb view ahead of you to the sea as you go. At the next T-junction, turn left.

Woodbury Common, along with six neighbouring commons, is part of the East Devon Pebblebed Heath, one of the largest surviving examples of lowland heath in the country, and a designated Site of Special Scientific Interest.

Ignore the track running off to the right just before you reach the plantation ahead of you, and the next one, which runs to the right into the plantation about 300 yards further on. Soon after the second track, you enter the plantation yourself, and 300 yards beyond it you will come to another junction, marked by a blue waymark on a post; turn right here down a path. This takes you into a beautiful area of gorse and trees, mainly broadleaves, but with the conifers of the plantation visible to your right. At the junction bear right, and at the next go straight on. You will come to a pole barrier; turn right beyond it and you will come out onto a road. (1¾ miles)

② Turn left and follow the road for about 500 yards into the hamlet of **Yettington**. Take the first lane on

THE SIR WALTER RALEIGH, EAST BUDLEIGH

the right (signposted to **Exmouth**). After 200 yards you will find a stile on the left, just beyond a gate; there is a public footpath sign, but it is somewhat hidden in the hedge. Cross the stile and keep to the left of the field beyond. Go through a gateway at the end and keep to the left of the next field. At the end go round to the right to reach a stile halfway along. The thatched farmhouse you can see on your right as you go is **Hayes Barton**, where Sir Walter Raleigh was born.

Cross the stile and turn left along the lane (or turn right if you want a proper view of **Hayes Barton**, but do bear in mind that it is a private house, and it is not open to the public). Follow the lane for about a mile to the pretty village of **East Budleigh**. (1¾ miles)

Born at Hayes Barton, Sir Walter Raleigh was educated at what was then the vicarage, now a lovely thatched house called Vicar's Mead, on the edge of East Budleigh. (As with Hayes Barton, however, the house is not open to the public, so please respect the privacy of the owners.)

③ **The Sir Walter Raleigh** pub is immediately opposite you when you reach the T-junction in the centre of the village, should you feel the need for some refreshment at this halfway stage in your walk.

To resume the walk, turn left as you leave the pub (right if you are emerging from **Hayes Lane**) and make your way through the village, with a stream on your left. When you come to the school, turn right up a little lane and through a farmyard to a green lane. There is an abundance of wild flowers in the hedgerows, but the lane itself can be muddy, so take care. After 500 yards you will come to a junction. If at this point there is a sign indicating that the road ahead is closed because of erosion, you may want to make a short detour. However, despite the warning it is quite passable for walkers with a bit of scrambling (and this is an adventurous walk, after all!). It is due to be repaired, but at the time of writing there was no sign of any work being done.

If you decide on the detour, turn right at the sign and follow another green lane for about 200 yards, then turn left onto a path to cross three fields and emerge on the original route higher up.

You get an excellent view across the farmland to the right from the top of the green lane and then it enters **Hayes Wood**, running between high banks along the edge of the trees. Ignore the first public footpath sign on the right, but at the next one, 300 yards beyond it, go half-right down a clear track. (1½ miles)

④ This track takes you through the

wood for a short distance and then goes left to leave it. This stretch is a mass of foxgloves and buddleia in summer. You go through a clearing and pass a pole barrier to a car park and road. Cross over, pass another pole barrier and go straight on, following the yellow waymark (do not follow the main track towards the right). The path runs alongside a wood on the right, with the open spaces of **East Budleigh common** on the left. At the top edge of the wood go right, following the waymark again. You come out at a road; turn right and follow it for about 150 yards. (3/4 mile)

⑤ You will see a public bridlepath sign on the left; turn off the road here and follow the path to the right and then left to skirt a deep quarry. This path twists and turns somewhat, and there are a number of paths and tracks leading off it, so you need to look out for the blue bridlepath waymarks which you will find on posts at regular intervals, usually accompanied by the foxglove emblem of the **East Devon Way**.

About 1/2 mile after leaving the road you will find that the way diverges; the blue waymark points left, while a pink arrow with the **East Devon Way** foxglove points straight on. Follow the latter. You will come to more junctions and turnings, but as long as you keep following the pink waymarks you will have no problems. Along this stretch you get a lovely view across the common to woods and farms on your right, and to the sea behind you.

The path comes out at a car park; cross it to a road and cross that, still following the **East Devon Way**. After a few yards the latter goes left to cross another road; leave it here and carry straight on, parallel to the road. This path takes you back to the **Woodbury Castle** car park after another 1/2 mile. (1 1/2 miles)

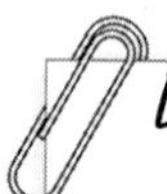

Date walk completed:

Walk 12

THE UNDERCLIFF: THE EAST DEVON COAST BETWEEN LYME REGIS AND AXMOUTH

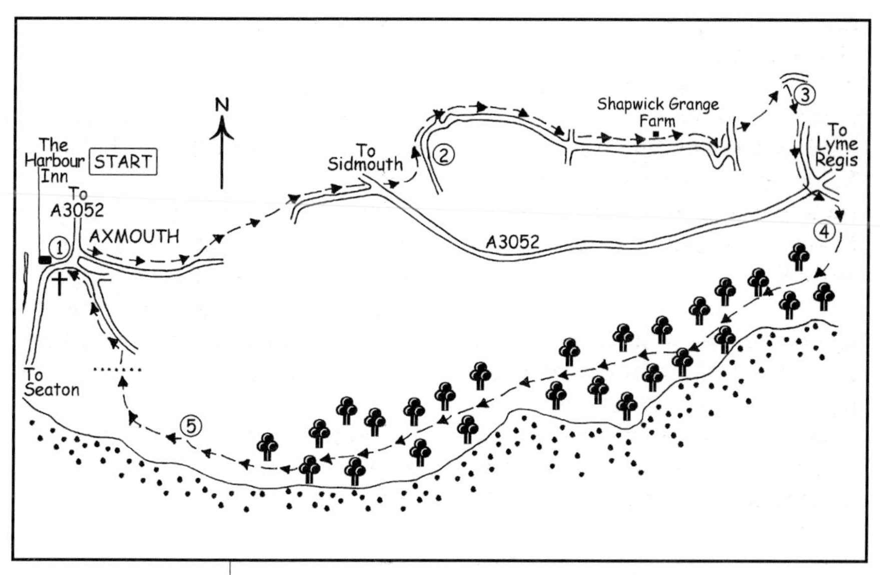

Distance:
11 miles

Starting point:
Axmouth, where there is parking on the main road. Parking is also available on Chapel Street, which runs east from the main road. GR 256911

Maps: OS Explorer 116 Lyme Regis and Bridport; OS Landranger 193 Taunton and Lyme Regis

How to get there: *Axmouth is on the B3172 just south of the A3052 Sidmouth to Lyme Regis road, and just north of Seaton.*

CANNINGTON VIADUCT

Combining quiet, flower-filled lanes, tracks and paths with the thick, lush vegetation of the Undercliff, this beautiful walk is a visual delight. And the pretty village of Axmouth, from which we start out, is an added attraction – so allow a bit of time to explore its lanes and church. The outward leg of the walk is relatively easy, with just a few fairly easy ascents. The return, along the Undercliff, is a bit rougher and can become muddy in places after rain, but there are few steep climbs to worry about.

Axmouth is believed to have been the southern terminus of the Fosse Way in Roman times, and it was one of the earliest Saxon villages to be established in this part of the country. Its value as a harbour began to wane in the Middle Ages, however, when a landslip formed a high pebble ridge across the estuary, almost barring access to the sea.

The Harbour Inn is a lovely pub that dates back to the days when Axmouth had a harbour. Reckoned to be over 800 years old, it has the original beams and fireplaces to prove it. It is larger than it looks from the road, comprising five rooms in addition to a large garden. The entrance from the car park opens straight into the delightful family room, which has a stone floor and wooden tables and benches. To the right of this room is a function room with the garden beyond; to the left are the bar, lounge and restaurant.

The bar is a warm, cosy room divided by wooden partitions into snug little alcoves, with an enormous stone fireplace at one end. It leads into the lounge, furnished with comfortable chairs and tables, with another enormous stone fireplace at the end. Beyond the lounge, and sharing its fireplace, is a lovely little restaurant, with an enormous dresser opposite the fireplace.

It is full of atmosphere and both locals and visitors receive a warm welcome.

The menu *varies from day to day, but there are always sandwiches and snacks available, as well as main courses. Telephone: 01297 20371.*

① To start the walk, head north-east along the main village street, towards the A3052 (so if, for example, you have parked in **Chapel Street** you should return to the main road and turn right). As you leave the village, turn right up **Higher Lane**. This will take you out of **Axmouth**, climbing as it goes. It is a pretty lane, especially in summer.

After 3/4 mile, you will see a clear, broad track leading off to the left; turn off and follow it. Like the lane, it is full of wild flowers in summer, and you get a very good view to the right across the valley. You continue to enjoy this view through gaps in the hedge for about 1/2 mile, until the track meets another lane. Go straight on, past a farm, to the main road.

Cross over to the drive for **Westhayes** and **Pinewood**, and turn immediately right through a gate into a field, following the direction of the public footpath sign. Keep to the left of the field beyond and go through the first gate at the end. Turn right and keep to the right of the next field. Follow the boundary round to the left until you come to a stile; cross it and bear left and then right through a belt of trees. Go down across a field to a gate. This leads into a little copse. Follow the path through it to a lane. (2 1/4 miles)

② Turn left, and at the junction 200

yards further on turn right (signposted to **Shapwick**). Follow this new lane for a little over 3/4 mile to a crossroads; go straight across (signposted to **Shapwick** again). Cross a cattle grid and go down into a valley. You pass some farm buildings and then go through a farmyard and past the attractive farmhouse of **Shapwick Grange Farm**. You will see the impressive **Cannington Viaduct** ahead of you to the left.

Completed in 1903, the Cannington Viaduct was part of the Axminster and Lyme Regis Light Railway. it was constructed entirely of concrete.

Continue along the lane past a drive and round to the right. It then turns very sharp left, with the entrance to a quarry straight ahead. Follow the lane round and you will come to a junction; turn left (signposted to **Holcombe** and **Uplyme**). You pass a house on your right. Just beyond it turn right through a gate, following the public bridleway sign. Now you get a very much closer view of the viaduct. Cross the field on the other side to a gate in the hedge ahead, which is marked with a pink waymark. The path on the other side leads to another gate. Beyond it you pass a house and come out onto a drive; go straight on. The drive emerges

THE HARBOUR INN, AXMOUTH

onto a lane at some cottages. (2¼ miles)

③ Just beyond the cottages you will find some steps on the right, marked with a public footpath sign. Climb them into a wood and turn right behind the cottages and then to the left, further into the wood. Leave the wood via a stile and keep to the left of the field beyond. Halfway along you will see a stile on the left; cross it and keep to the top of the next field, alongside a hedge. Cross another stile and then yet another one into a lane; bear right.

The lane comes out at the A3052; cross over to another lane (signposted to **Ware**). After 250 yards you will come to the drive for **Ware Farm** on the right; turn up it and then almost immediately left across a stile, following the public footpath sign. Follow the track on the other side round to the right, following the yellow waymark. At the end continue along the path to the left and cross a stile, still following the waymarks. Keep to the left of the field on the other side to another stile, which leads you into the dense woodland of the **Undercliff**. (1 mile)

This stretch of coast has been subject to landslips for some time. The most traumatic occurred on Christmas night 1839 when a large part of the Dowland Cliff collapsed, taking with it fields and trees, and demolishing cottages. During the course of the night, over 20 acres of land had sunk, some of it coming to rest halfway down the cliff and the rest falling into a ravine ¾ mile long.

For obvious reasons, the area became known as the Undercliff. The environment is almost tropical in the speed and lushness with which the vegetation grows – facing south, sheltered from the cold north wind and with the slope of the displaced land at just the right angle to make the most of the sun's rays. The year after the Dowland slip it was possible to harvest a whole field of wheat that had fallen into the Undercliff, but after that nature took over, and woodland quickly established itself. It is now a national nature reserve, and although it is safe to walk along the waymarked route, there is dangerous terrain on either side so care is needed.

④ Go steeply down some steps and at the bottom of the cliff, cross a footbridge. At the fork, bear right and go down to a broad, well-worn path. This is the **South West Coast Path**. Turn right along it.

In the 18th and 19th centuries, smuggling was a major source of income for the communities along Devon's south coast, and the shoreline of East Devon was the

perfect terrain for it. The cliffs provided shelter for the smugglers landing their contraband, the caves were ideal for hiding it, and there were numerous hidden paths through the dense undergrowth of the Undercliff along which they could distribute it, and along which they could ambush any pursuing excisemen. As one sticks closely to the safety of the path, one can imagine how easy it was for the smugglers, who knew this coast like the backs of their hands, to conceal themselves – and how dangerous it could be for the poor excisemen.

About 1 mile after joining the Coast Path, you pass a pumping station; turn right beyond it, as indicated by the signpost, and continue along the path as it climbs through the wood. After another 3/4 mile you descend steeply to a track; turn left and follow it to the right, then leave it to follow the Coast Path sign to the left.

Roughly a mile after leaving the track, and just when you are beginning to wonder whether the thick undergrowth is going to last for ever, you emerge into more open country and get a lovely view across the Axe estuary to **Seaton**. The path now runs through a patch of scrub and climbs away from the coast, alternating between thick bush and open country – and whenever you reach the latter you are met by that superb view across to **Seaton**. You finally climb steeply to a stile. (4 miles)

⑤ You are now on the homeward stretch, so take a few moments to catch your breath before crossing the stile and bearing left. The path now runs along the top of the cliff and you continue to enjoy an excellent view across the estuary. After about 1/4 mile, bear right along a clear path, following the yellow waymarks. At the end, follow the path to the left through a gateway and then to the right. Keep to the right-hand side of a field and at the end go right and then left onto a path between high hedges.

You come to a track; cross it to a stile (signposted to **Axmouth**). You now get a lovely view across the **Axe valley** to your left. Go straight across a field to another stile, leading into a lane. Turn left and follow the lane as it descends quite steeply to **Axmouth**. At the T-junction turn left again. You are now in **Chapel Street**; at the end turn left again to reach the **Harbour Inn** and a well-deserved drink! (1 1/2 miles)

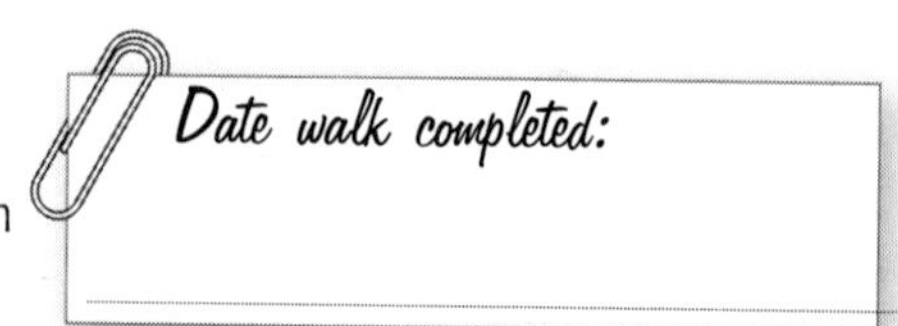

Walk 13

ANCIENT RITUALS: A MERRIVALE CIRCUIT

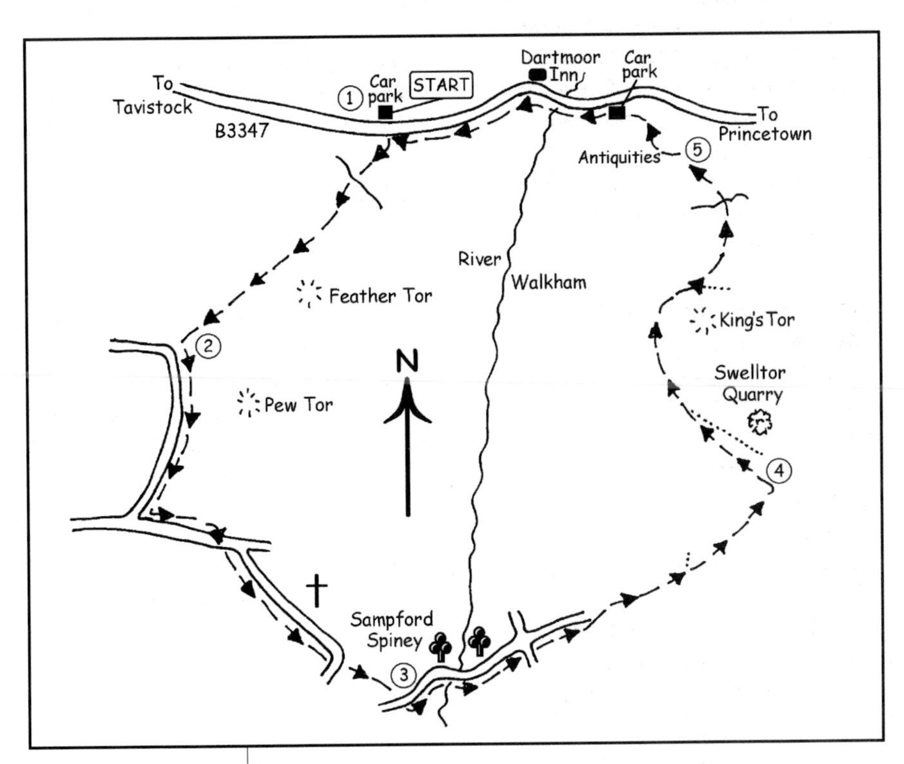

Distance:
7 miles

Starting point:
The western parking area at Merrivale. GR 539750

Maps: OS Explorer OL28 Dartmoor; OS Landranger 191 Okehampton and North Dartmoor

How to get there: *Merrivale is on the B3347 between Tavistock and Princetown. The route directions start from a parking area on the northern side of the road, a little over 1/2 mile west of Merrivale Bridge and the Dartmoor Inn, so that you visit the pub at the end of the walk, when you have worked up a thirst. If you would like to call in at the pub at the start of the walk, there is another parking area on the southern side of the road, at the top of the hill to the east of Merrivale Bridge.*

This superb walk gives you a taste of Dartmoor without too much effort. You can experience the feeling of space that is such a feature of the high moor, the magnificent skies and the almost tangible silence, with extensive views for much of the route. There is also a great deal of interest along the way, from a disused quarry to an ancient ritual site. There is a stiff climb in the middle of the walk and another, considerably shorter and easier, at the end, but otherwise it is all easy going.

The Dartmoor Inn is a well-preserved, 17th-century building, which was originally a row of cottages. It comprises a long lounge bar with an enormous granite fireplace at one end, and a snug public bar leading off it. The lounge has an interesting collection of chinaware, with plates along the walls and jugs, mugs, teapots and even chamber pots hanging from the beams. There is also seating outside, with sweeping views over the River Walkham and Dartmoor.

The pub *is renowned for its country wines and real ales, as well as the quality of its food. The latter ranges from ploughman's lunches, salads and soups to main courses such as lasagne, Cumberland sausage and steaks.*
Telephone 01822 890340.

① Starting from the western parking area, cross the road and make your way down the hill on the other side. After 100 yards or so you will come to a path crossing in front of you; turn right along it (if you miss it, don't worry – simply head to the right of **Feather Tor**, the loose collection of rocks you can see on the horizon half-right). Follow the path across a leat and down to a stream; cross it and bear left along the path on the other side. The moorland views start straight away, and now that you are away from the road you will notice the silence.

About 500 yards after crossing the stream you will come to a cross. This is an old route marker. You cross another leat, just where it forks. The path runs downhill between the two branches to a wall

THE PRETTY HAMLET OF SAMPFORD SPINEY

and then goes alongside it to a lane. It is not as clear here as it was earlier, but if you are in any doubt, just turn right and make your way down through the gorse until you reach a wall. Then turn left along it and follow it round until you meet the lane. As you go down, you have a very good outlook over the farmland of what is called the 'in country', the area on the fringes of the moor. (1 mile)

② Turn left and follow the lane for about 1/2 mile to a T-junction; turn left again (signposted to **Sampford Spiney**). As you go, you continue to get some lovely views across to the right and ahead. After another 700 yards you will come to another junction; turn right and follow another lane into the hamlet of **Sampford Spiney**.

At the next T-junction, bear right. Over the wall on the right you continue to get a good view across Dartmoor. You pass **Stoneycroft**, a large and attractive house, on the left, and the lane curves to the right. As it does so, go straight on along a green lane, which is signposted as unsuitable for motor vehicles. (1 3/4 miles)

③ You emerge onto another lane by a cattle grid; turn left and cross the cattle grid. The lane enters a pretty wood and descends between high walls before swinging to the right to cross the **River Walkham** at **Ward Bridge**. It then climbs up the other side of the valley. It is a fairly long and stiff climb, but the views from the top are worth it. After 500 yards you come to a crossroads; go straight on, still climbing (signposted to **Criptor**). At the top you cross a cattle grid and emerge onto the open moor.

As I promised, the panorama that now opens up makes the effort of the climb worthwhile. A range of tors come into view, starting on the left with **Great Staple Tor** on the horizon and **Vixen Tor** lower down, then **King's Tor** half-left in the middle ground, **Swelltor Quarry** straight ahead and **Ingra Tor**, the closest, on the right. Follow a track to a gate in a wall and go through. Continue along the track on the other side. When it goes to the left follow it round and after a few yards leave it to follow the direction of a public bridlepath sign on the right.

It indicates a path that winds through the gorse. Follow it, looking

THE DARTMOOR INN

out for the blue bridlepath waymarks to point the way, some of them on posts, some of them just dots painted on rocks. You cross a stream and about 600 yards after leaving the track you come to a gate in a fence. Go through and you will find yourself on the track of the **Plymouth and Dartmoor Railway**. ($1^3/_4$ miles)

In the late 18th century, Sir Thomas Tyrwhitt, friend of the Prince Regent and owner of Tor Royal, near what is now Princetown, had a dream: to open up and 'civilise' this part of Dartmoor. A major part of his plan was a railway to link Princetown with Plymouth. This railway (in fact, it was a horse-drawn tramway) was to bring lime and sea sand to Dartmoor to improve the soil and return to Plymouth with granite. Sadly, the venture proved a flop. Although the line was later converted to steam, it was finally closed in 1956.

④ Turn left and follow the broad track as it contours round below **Swelltor**. You get the best view yet as you look out to the left, over the moor and the country beyond as far as Cornwall on a clear day. Above you are the quarry spoil tips. If you want to see the quarry itself (and it is an impressive and interesting sight), you should cut up right after about $^1/_4$ mile or so to another track, a branch line of the old railway, and the quarry entrance beyond. Alternatively, you can follow the track you are on for $^1/_2$ mile to the junction with the branch line and follow the latter back.

Swelltor was among several granite quarries on Dartmoor, most of them in the Princetown/ Merrivale area. The last to close was Merrivale itself, the remains of which can be seen above the hamlet; this did not close until 1997. They supplied granite for some of the major public buildings in London and elsewhere, including London Bridge, Covent Garden, the British Museum and the National Gallery.

Not far from Swelltor Quarry can be found some enormous corbels, just lying alongside the dismantled railway branch line, about 100 yards or so from its junction with the main line. These were cut and carved for the widening of London Bridge at the start of the 20th century, but were found to be surplus to requirements and now adorn the open moor!

A little way beyond the junction between the branch line and the main line the track goes across an embankment and then through a cutting, curving to the right as it does so. When you emerge from the cutting you will see a wall below you. Carry on along the track until you can see the corner of the wall, then cut down through the gorse to it. When you reach it, follow the wall round to the left. Towards the bottom, bear right slightly away from it to cross a stream at a ford. Follow the clear path on the other side to an upright stone you can see on the horizon. This is one of the marker stones for the ancient **Tavistock** to **Ashburton packhorse trail**. You can see the 'T' for Tavistock and the 'A' for Ashburton on opposite sides of the stone. (1½ miles)

⑤ Turn left at the stone and head towards the remains of **Merrivale Quarry**, which can be seen across the valley. You will soon come to the first of the stone rows for which **Merrivale** is famous.

The Merrivale antiquities comprise the largest and most diverse ritual site on Dartmoor, with three stone rows (one of which is now difficult to identify since it consists of only three stones), a stone circle (not very well preserved) and a standing stone. There are also a number of cairns and a kistvaen (a small burial chamber without a cairn covering it). They all date from what is known as the Beaker Period, around 2500 – 2000 BC. To the right of the site, near to the road, there are the remains of several Bronze Age huts.

As you follow the stone row you will see the standing stone and stone circle on the left. Closer to is the kistvaen, with the burial chamber exposed by the collapse of the central covering stone. Go right almost opposite it to the hut remains, and when you have finished there turn left and follow the line of the road to the eastern parking area. From here you will have a welcome view: the **Dartmoor Inn** at the bottom of the hill. Follow the road down and across the bridge to the pub.

Continue along the road and up the hill on the other side. Just over ½ mile beyond the pub, you will find the western parking area on your right. (1 mile)

Walk 14

WHERE FALCONS FLY: HALDON HILL, DODDISCOMBSLEIGH AND ASHTON

THE NOBODY INN, DODDISCOMBSLEIGH

Distance:
7 miles

Starting point:
The Bullens Hill car park in Haldon Forest. GR 881847

Maps: OS Explorer 110 Torquay and Dawlish; OS Landranger 192 Exeter and Sidmouth (start and finish), 191 Okehampton and North Dartmoor (middle section)

How to get there: *Haldon Forest straddles the A38 and A380 a few miles south of Exeter. Turn west off the A38 at the top of Haldon Hill (or the A380 at the top of Telegraph Hill), following the signs for Dunchideock. The Bullens Hill car park is about 1¼ miles from the A38 and is clearly marked.*

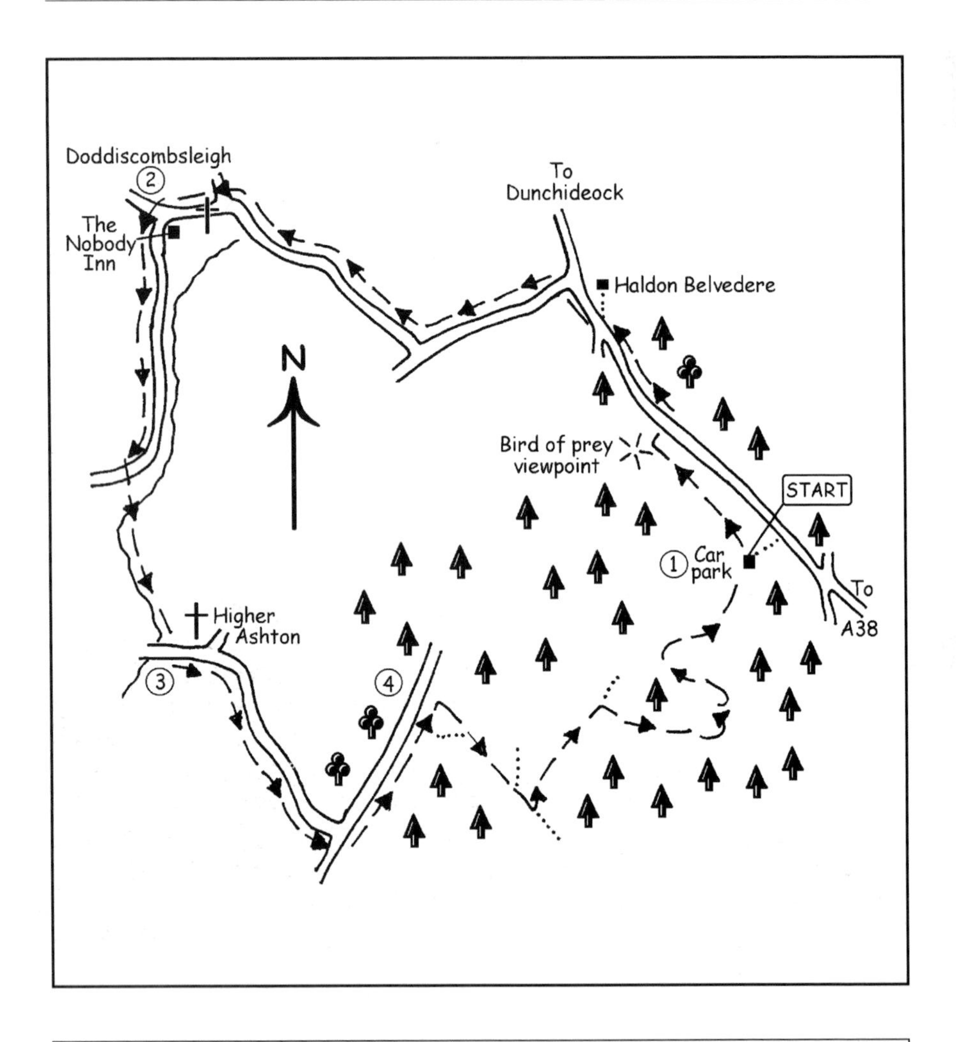

This is a walk of quiet, little-used woodland lanes, shady forest tracks and lovely views – some of them quite spectacular and made all the more attractive by the suddenness with which they appear. It is a delightful exploration of this tranquil little corner of Devon, which, despite its proximity to Exeter and the busy Devon Expressway, seems to belong to a different era. There are one or two fairly stiff climbs, but they are quite short.

The Nobody Inn, in Doddiscombsleigh, is a delightful 16th-century inn. It derives its unusual name from a local legend, according to which a previous owner locked the place up and refused to open the doors to travellers who came knocking. They therefore went on their way in the belief that there was 'nobody in'. You need have no fear of that happening today. Visitors are sure of a warm welcome and award-winning food. The inn is full of atmosphere, with ancient beams and leaded windows. The bar has an enormous inglenook fireplace and comfortable settles and chairs. Outside is a patio. Unfortunately, they do not have a children's licence, so children are only allowed on the patio.

The pub *is particularly noted for its local cheeses – indeed, all the dishes are prepared from local produce where possible. It is also noted for its whiskies and wines – over 200 whiskies and some 700 wines are available – and its local cider and traditional beers. Telephone: 01647 252394.*

① Head towards the exit of the car park. Just beyond the end of the parking area you will find a grassy path leading off to the left; follow it. You immediately get a superb view to the left, over the **Teign Valley** to **Dartmoor**. The path dips and the trees close in around it. It becomes fairly muddy but soon dries out again. At some points it is quite narrow, but always passable. When you come to a junction in the path turn left and after a few yards you will come to a wooden barrier on your right; go through it and at the top turn left to go to the bird of prey viewpoint or right to continue the walk.

This viewpoint is a superb place from which to view both resident and migrating raptors. The thermals are ideal for them, and the hunting is good. You can see a wide variety of birds, including buzzards, honey buzzards, goshawks, hobbies, sparrowhawks, peregrines and kestrels. If you are lucky and choose the right time of year you might also see migrating red kites and ospreys. This is also an ideal place to enjoy the incredible views across the South Devon countryside. Note: Dogs are not allowed at the viewpoint.

Go through the viewpoint car park to a road. Turn left and follow it as it bends to the right among some trees and begins to descend. At the junction go straight on (signposted to **Exeter**). After a few yards you will find the entrance to **Haldon Belvedere** on the right. The views from the belvedere are breathtaking – to **Exeter** and beyond on one side and across woods and farms to **Dartmoor** on the other.

The triangular tower, known as both Haldon Belvedere and Lawrence Castle was built in 1788 by Sir Robert Palk, former Governor of Madras and owner of the Haldon estate, in memory of Major-General Stringer Lawrence, commander of the East India Company's troops in the 18th century. He was known as the 'father of the Indian Army', and there is a statue of him.

HALDON BELVEDERE

Continue along the road for 300 yards to the next junction and turn left (signposted to **Ashton** and **Doddiscombsleigh**). The view of Dartmoor is now ahead of you, and occasionally through the hedge on your right you can see the patchwork of fields and hedges that is so typical of the countryside around here. It is a lovely, quiet, tree-fringed lane which winds down quite steeply initially and then levels off. After a little under 1/2 mile there is a further junction; turn right. This is another pretty lane, which winds down through a wood. Suddenly another very attractive view opens up ahead of you. At the next junction go straight on (signposted to **Christow**) to enter the delightful little village of **Doddiscombsleigh** and you will find the equally delightful **Nobody Inn** on your left after 300 yards – and who could resist stopping at a hostelry with such an intriguing name? (2 1/2 miles)

② Turn left as you leave the pub, and at the junction left again (signposted to **Ashton**). This is yet another lovely lane, fringed by trees initially and then by flower-filled hedgerows, and with the **Shippen Brook** gliding along on your left, sometimes alongside the lane, sometimes a little distance away. After about 1/2 mile the lane bends to the right and then straightens out. After another 200 yards or so it curves to the right again and begins to climb. As it does so, look out for a public footpath sign on the left just beyond some farm buildings.

Turn off here, go through a gate and then diagonally right across the field on the other side. There is no clear path, but you should aim for the far right-hand corner. Go through a gap in the hedge on the right when you get there, and then turn left to cross a footbridge. Turn right on the other side and keep a short distance from the brook to a gate in the fence ahead. This leads into a lovely, cool wood. Follow the clear path through it until you come to a gate into a field. Go to the left and follow the path alongside it, with the wood still on your left.

When you come to a fence ahead of you cross a stile on the right and turn left to continue along the path between two fences. Cross another stile at the end into a field, and keep to the path along the left-hand boundary. Go through a gate onto a track and follow that to another gate. Pass a farm on your right and go through a third gate onto a lane. (1¼ miles)

③ Turn left and follow the lane to **Higher Ashton**. At the junction, go straight on (signposted to **Trusham**) or turn left and then immediately left again to visit **Ashton Church**.

Ashton Church has been described as the most beautiful church in Devon. It still has many of its medieval features, including carved benches and a wall-painting. Some of the glass is also medieval, and the pulpit is Elizabethan – you can still see the original hourglass and sounding board.

The lane goes down to a stream, then swings to the right and to the left and climbs up a steep hill. After ¼ mile or so it levels off and bends to the right and to the left again. I'm afraid the climbing isn't quite over yet, however: the lane now climbs for another 200 yards to a T-junction. Turn left.

Although this lane still climbs, the ascent is so gentle you will hardly notice it. And it is a lovely stretch, with woodland on either side. After ½ mile you will see the entrance to an airstrip on the left. A few yards beyond it is a gate on the right leading into **Haldon Forest**. (1¼ miles)

④ Go through the gap alongside the gate onto a track and follow it down into the forest. At the first junction, go straight on along the main track. About ¼ mile further on, your track joins a much clearer one; bear right. At the next junction, about 100 yards further on, turn left. This is a broad track which climbs towards the top of the forest. You don't follow it all the way, however. After 600 yards you will come to another track going right; take that. From time to time as you follow it you will come across posts painted with a blue stripe; these are markers for one of the forest's waymarked walks and will accompany you for the rest of the route.

Keep to this track for about 1/2 mile (in fact the blue waymarks are hardly necessary, as there is nowhere else to go). When it ends go straight on along a path, which winds and climbs, then crosses a boardwalk, all the time marked with the blue-painted posts. At the top there is a junction. Follow the waymarks to the left. This is a particularly pretty stretch in early summer, as the path is lined with rhododendrons. You pass several barriers designed to deter cyclists, climbing all the time, and the rhododendrons give way to conifers.

Then, quite unexpectedly, the trees clear on the left and you can once again enjoy the amazing panorama over the **Teign Valley** to **Dartmoor**, with **Haytor** half-left on the horizon. In this cleared area the ground is carpeted with gorse and heather, forming a lovely patchwork of yellow and purple in late summer. The path now swings sharply to the right and enters the trees again. You cross a track and then, a little later, go down some steps and cross another. Follow the waymark on the other side and after a few yards you will meet another, broader path. Turn right (signposted 'Return to car park'). When this path forks go left and you will soon come to a steep path leading up to the car park on your right. (2 miles)

Walk 15

UNCLE TOM COBLEY AND OTHER FOLK: WIDECOMBE, HOUND TOR AND HAMEL DOWN

THE OLD INN, WIDECOMBE IN THE MOOR

Distance:
$9\frac{1}{2}$ miles

Starting point:
Either of the two public car parks signposted in Widecombe. GR 719768

Maps: OS Explorer OL28 Dartmoor; OS Landranger 191 Okehampton and North Dartmoor

How to get there: *Widecombe in the Moor can be found at the end of the B3387, which runs west from the A382 at Bovey Tracey.*

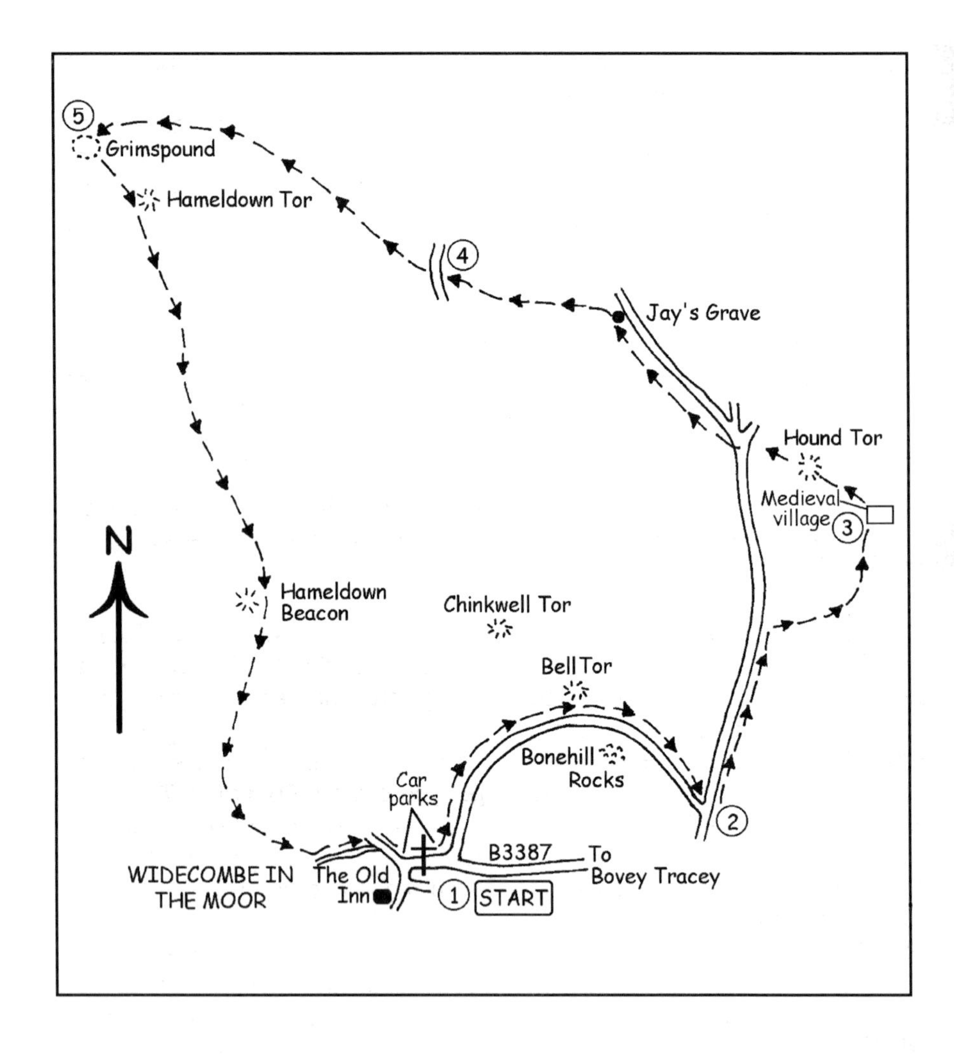

The views around Widecombe will take your breath away, and they are a major feature of this route. There is also a great deal of other interest along the way – ruins of settlements dating from the Bronze Age and medieval times, a grave with a story, and legends galore. It is not a walk for the unfit, however. The views come at a price; there are a few steep climbs to negotiate before you can enjoy them.

The Old Inn is a lovely granite hostelry dating from the 14th century – and it shows. It is quite a large establishment, with a number of cosy, snug rooms: two bars, a lounge, two dining rooms, all carpeted, and a family room with a stone floor. All are tastefully decorated, and have exposed granite walls. Outside is a delightful large garden with a number of water features. And despite the number of visitors Widecombe sees each year, it is happily uncommercialised; it is as charming and full of atmosphere as many less frequented village inns.

The food *is varied and of a very high standard. You might like to try their mixed grill, which they claim is world famous – and given the number of foreign tourists they entertain, that is probably no idle boast! Telephone: 01364 621207.*

The Walk

① As you leave the car park (whichever one you use), turn left. At the end of the village green you will see a stone pillar, on the top of which is a depiction of **Uncle Tom Cobley** and his companions on their way to Widecombe Fair.

The folk song 'Widecombe Fair', with its famous refrain, 'Uncle Tom Cobley and All' is based on a character who actually existed, as did all his companions – although whether they really did all try to ride to Widecombe Fair on the same horse is uncertain! They came from a village called Spreyton, just north of South Tawton on the northern edge of Dartmoor, and the grave of Tom Cobley (or Cobleigh) can be seen in the churchyard there.

Widecombe Fair is still held every year, on the second Tuesday in September.

Follow the lane out of the village, and take the first turning on the left. This pretty lane bends to the right to cross a stream and then you begin the first of the climbs. As you go, you can see **Chinkwell Tor** and **Bell Tor** beckoning ahead of you. You eventually emerge onto the open moor, and you will find **Bonehill Rocks** immediately on your right. This is a favourite place for children, who love scrambling on the rocks. If you are tempted (and have the energy!) to do the same, just remember that the walk has hardly started. Instead, you might be better to take a breather while you enjoy the first of the views – a superb panorama on the right over the farms and dry stone walls to open moorland in the distance.

Continue along the lane as it

winds to the right and to the left. As you swing left you get another excellent view, with a range of tors spread out ahead of you, from **Haytor** on the left to **Pil Tor** on the right. (1¼ miles)

② At the T-junction turn left. This road can be quite busy, but there is a path alongside it on the left if you need to get away from the traffic. The moor around you is ablaze with gorse and heather in late summer. After a little over ½ mile you cross a cattle grid, and 150 yards beyond that you will come to a gate and stile on the right, with a sign pointing to **Hound Tor Down** and **Haytor Down**. Cross the stile and follow the clear path through the bracken, still with a good view of the range of tors on your right.

At the junction go straight on (signposted to **Hound Tor Down**). Go through a gap in a wall and turn left. As you do so you get another delightful view up ahead, across the densely wooded **Bovey Valley**. Go through a gate and to the left of **Greator Rocks**, which are just in front of you. Leave the rocks behind you and go down to the ruins of a medieval village below, which was abandoned, probably in the 15th century. (1½ miles)

ST PANCRAS CHURCH AT WIDECOMBE, THE 'CATHEDRAL OF THE MOOR'

③ Turn left and take the clear path up to **Hound Tor**, with the lovely view across the **Bovey Valley** on your right. When you get to the tor, you can either go round the bottom or through the central 'avenue' between the two rock outcrops. Once again, you would be advised to resist the temptation to climb the rocks themselves – you are less than a third of the way round the route!

On the other side of the tor bear right, aiming for the road junction just to the left of the **Hound Tor** car park. At the junction turn right (signposted to **Manaton**, **Moretonhampstead** and **Chagford**). You pass an attractive thatched cottage; at the junction just beyond, follow the main road to the left. After another 1/2 mile or so, you will find a grave on your left; this is **Jay's Grave**.

The grave is said to contain the skeleton of Kitty (or Mary) Jay who, in the 17th century, committed suicide and so was buried in an unmarked grave at a crossroads to prevent her spirit returning to haunt the living. Interestingly, the grave always has fresh flowers on it. Tradition has it that they are left by the pixies.

Turn left at the grave and go through a gate onto a path between banks (signposted to **Natsworthy**). Follow this pretty lane, with good views to the left, for about 3/4 mile to another gate, leading into a lane. (1 3/4 miles)

④ Turn left and almost immediately right through another gate. At the junction on the other side, go straight on (signposted to the road near **Firth Bridge**). Follow the broad path to the right as it follows the forest boundary round. Where the path forks go left to climb up the side of a ridge. You will come to a path junction. On the left is a large stone commemorating the crew of an RAF aeroplane which crashed here during the Second World War, killing all on board.

Go straight across the junction, and at the top of the ridge pause to enjoy the lovely view to your right and behind you. As you come over the brow you will see **Hookney Tor** ahead of you. The path curves down to the left of the tor, and as it does so, yet another superb panorama opens up in front of you. You then descend gently to the enclosure of **Grimspound**. If you are looking for somewhere to stop for a picnic, you could do worse than to find a suitable rock here on which to perch and enjoy the view across the valley in front of you. (1 1/2 miles)

During the Bronze Age, there were a great many settlements on Dartmoor – the remains of over 4,000 huts dating from that period have been found. The walls of the huts at Grimspound were about 4 ft high, and up to 8 ft thick to provide maximum insulation. The roof was thatched, using heather, rushes or bracken.

The surrounding wall of the settlement was originally about 10 ft high, and was there to protect the livestock from predators rather than serve any defensive purpose.

⑤ Turn left at **Grimspound**, go through a gap in the outer wall and follow the path that climbs steeply up the hill. As you come to the top look to the left for a magnificent view over the moor to the patchwork of farm fields and woods beyond. The path takes you to **Hameldown Tor**, where there is a cairn. From there you follow a clear, broad path leading along the ridge of **Hamel Down**, with the most incredible views to the right and then also to the left. Moreover you can appreciate them all the more knowing that there is no more climbing to do!

You pass the remains of **Hamel Down Cross**, a wayside cross that now has only one arm, and then a succession of ancient burial mounds: **Broad Barrow**, **Single Barrow** and **Two Barrows**. You then find a wall on your right, and at the end is the cairn of **Hameldown Beacon**. The views to left and right are now connected by an equally impressive one straight ahead, giving you a stunning 180° panorama.

Soon after passing **Hameldown Beacon** you start to descend, and as you come down off the ridge you get a good view half left over **Widecombe**. From this viewpoint you can see how **Widecombe church** got its name of 'the Cathedral of the Moor'; its impressive high tower dominates the surrounding area. You will come to a wall on your left; follow the path alongside it, and as it goes left go half-left, following the path sign. The path takes you down to a gate leading into a green lane. This comes out at a surfaced lane; bear left. At the T-junction at the bottom of the hill turn right to return to the village. The car parks are to the left, but if you feel in need of refreshment after your efforts you may prefer to turn right to the **Old Inn**. ($3\frac{1}{2}$ miles)

A popular Dartmoor legend tells of a Widecombe tin miner by the name of Jan Reynolds, who sold his soul to the Devil. One stormy Sunday in 1638 Old Dewer, as he is called in these parts, came to collect his due. Jan was in church; so the Devil tied his horse to the church tower and came crashing through the roof in a blaze of fire and brimstone. He grabbed Jan, sprang back up through the roof, threw him across his horse's back and disappeared into the stormy sky. That was the last that was seen of poor Jan Reynolds.

Some people have a more prosaic explanation of what happened on that day. They say that during the violent storm a fireball hit the church, destroying part of the roof and killing some of the congregation.

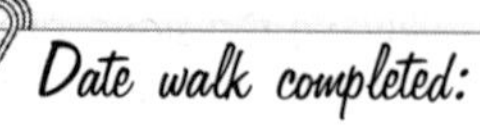

Walk 16

MONKS, TINNERS AND AN EVIL SQUIRE: HOLNE MOOR, BUCKFAST AND HEMBURY WOODS

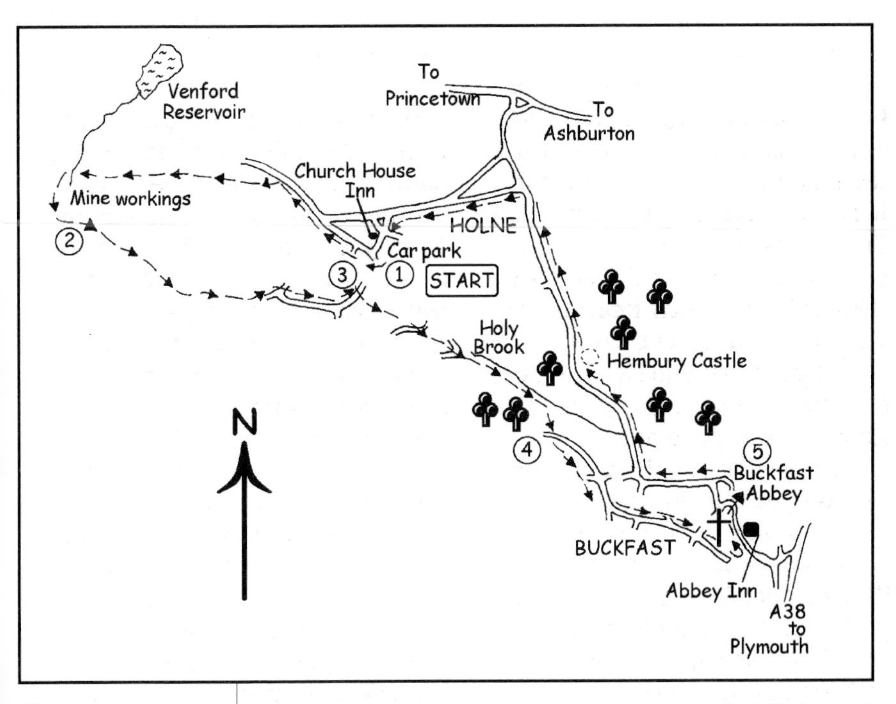

Distance:
11½ miles

Starting point:
Holne. There is a free public car park clearly signposted from the centre of Holne. GR 706694

Maps: OS Explorer OL28 Dartmoor; OS Landranger 202 Torbay and South Dartmoor

How to get there: *You can reach Holne either by turning south off the Ashburton to Princetown road between Holne Bridge and New Bridge and following the signs, or by leaving the A38 Devon Expressway at the Dart Bridge exit (signposted to Buckfast going north and Buckfastleigh going south) and again following the signs for Holne.*

This varied route offers you open moorland, farm tracks, woodland and riverside paths and deserted lanes, along with the chance to visit sites of great historical and social interest – all accompanied by some stunning views. Unfortunately, such delights carry a price: there are one or two hills along the way, but the lovely scenery through which you will be climbing makes even those a pleasure rather than a chore.

The Abbey Inn, halfway round the route, occupies an idyllic situation. Once ensconced on its terrace overlooking the River Dart, you may not want to leave again! It is an 18th-century building which has had several incarnations – first as Black Rock House, the home of the owner of the quarry across the road, then as a tea room and finally, in the 1970s, as a fully licensed pub.

It comprises three rooms, all beautifully panelled and decorated with prints: a bar as you enter and two interconnecting dining rooms. There is a large fireplace with a wood-burning stove in winter. Outside is the long terrace high above the river, from where you can watch the wildlife – 74 species of bird have been seen on the pub's property, as well as otters, badgers and deer.

The food *is wide-ranging, from bar meals to an interesting selection of main courses, including local fish. Telephone: 01364 642343.*

① Turn left as you leave the car park and at the junction follow the main lane round to the right (signposted to **Hexworthy** and **Michelcombe**). At the next junction go straight on, and at the next bear left (signposted to **Hexworthy**). The lane climbs up towards the open moor; as you climb you can look out over the hedge on the right across farms and woods to the moorland beyond, with **Rippon Tor** on the horizon.

Cross a cattle grid at the top and pass a disused quarry. Shortly after it you will see a track leading off to the left; follow it. It crosses a leat and then forks; take the right-hand branch. You now get a superb view over the **Dart valley** on the right. Cross another leat, a dried up one this time, and then about 200 yards further on another flowing one. As you climb, another panorama opens

THE ABBEY INN, BUCKFAST

up half-right. You are now probably following in the footsteps of medieval monks, as this is reckoned to be the rough route of the **Monks' Path**, used to cross the moor from Buckfast to Tavistock Abbey.

Soon **Venford** reservoir comes into view on the right, and as it does so the track becomes a grassy path. You cross a stream (**Venford Brook**) and then, about 200 yards further on, the path swings to the left to cross a deep gully, called a girt, made by the tin miners of old.

The path soon crosses another girt and curves right and then left, with yet another girt running parallel to it a few yards to the left. As you come over the rise, there is another extensive view ahead across the valley of the **River Mardle**. On the ridge you will find a grassy track crossing your path; turn left. (2¼ miles)

② As you follow this track you continue to enjoy the view over the Dart to the left, with the distinctive shape of **Haytor** on the horizon, but it is now almost overshadowed by what you can see up ahead – a patchwork of farm fields and woods that stretches all the way to the estuary of the **River Exe**. And it just gets better as the track begins to descend and more of it comes into view. You now also get a good view to the right.

When the track forks towards the

end of the ridge go right and descend to cross a dried up leat. About 150 yards beyond it you come to a gate; follow the track on the other side (signposted to **Michelcombe**). After about 1/2 mile you emerge through a gateway into a lane; go straight on. You soon come to a junction; turn right (signposted to **Scorriton** and **Buckfastleigh**). Follow this pretty lane down and to the left, and at the T-junction after about 600 yards go left (signposted to **Holne**). You pass **Littlecombe Farm** on the right and the lane curves to the left; as it does so, you will find a gate on the right, with a footpath sign to the county road at **Langaford**. (2 miles)

③ Go through the gate and keep to the right of the field beyond. Cross a stile at the end and keep to the right of the next field to reach a gate. Keep to the left of the next field, cross a stile at the end and go down some steps to a green lane. Cross it to a gate, following the direction of the public footpath sign. Keep alongside the fence on your right and at the end cross a stile to a paved courtyard. Cross that to a gate and turn right down a short drive, which brings you to a lane; turn left.

After 100 yards or so you will find a gate on your right with a footpath sign to **Mill Leat** and **Buckfast**. Go through it and follow the path amongst some trees on the right-hand side of a field, and then bear left along the bottom of a bracken-covered slope. Ignore the paths that go off to the right towards the stream at the bottom, and at the end you will come to a stile; cross it and continue along the path to a gate. Turn right along the lane on the other side and follow it down the hill. When it swings right at the bottom, turn left (signposted to **Burchetts Lodge** for **Buckfast**). You cross a footbridge and enter a lovely wood. This is a delightful stretch and you may like to linger, perhaps over a picnic, to watch the birds and enjoy the effect of the sun dappling the water of the Holy Brook, which runs alongside the path.

All too soon, after 1/2 mile or so, you leave the brook and climb to a track. Turn left and follow the track to a gate, which leads onto a drive. Follow that to a lane. (1 1/2 miles)

④ Turn left. At the crossroads after about 600 yards go straight on (signposted to **Buckfast** and **Buckfastleigh**). At the next junction go straight on again (signposted just to **Buckfastleigh** this time), and at the next one straight on again (again signposted to **Buckfast** as well as **Buckfastleigh**). About 250 yards beyond that you come to a junction with a main road; go straight on along a lane marked with a 'no through road' sign. This brings you to the churchyard and ruins of **Holy Trinity Church**, which burned down in 1992. Go through the lychgate and into the churchyard.

A few yards from the church entrance is the massive tomb of Richard Cabell, a particularly wicked local squire who was said to have sold his soul to the devil. When he died in 1677 he was buried under an enormous stone slab to ensure that he remained in his grave, and the large building you can see now was constructed around it. He was a great huntsman, and it is said that a pack of black phantom hounds come howling round his tomb on stormy nights. One legend has it that his ghost comes out and hunts across the moor from time to time, and anyone who sees it will die within a year.

Continue through the churchyard to a small gate at the end and go down some steps to a green lane. Turn left and follow it down to the right. You will see a rather dilapidated gate ahead of you; just before you reach it, swing left and carry on down the hill. You come out at a surfaced drive; bear right and follow it down to a main road, just by a roundabout. Turn left (signposted to **Buckfastleigh**, **Buckfast**, **Scorriton** and **Holne**). After 200 yards or so you will find the **Abbey Inn** on your right – a delightful place to break your walk and refresh yourself.

When you leave the inn turn right and follow the road for another 1/4 mile to a roundabout. Go straight on through a gateway, which takes you into the grounds of **Buckfast Abbey**. (Note: dogs are not allowed in the Abbey complex. If you have a dog you should turn left at the roundabout, follow the road up the hill and past the vehicle entrance to the Abbey. Turn right soon afterwards (signposted to **Buckfast**), and go down to a T-junction to rejoin the main route.) (2 1/4 miles)

The first abbey on this site was established in 1018, during the reign of King Knut (Canute). The present abbey took 32 years to build and was completed in

BUCKFAST ABBEY CHURCH

1938. One of the monks was a stonemason and with the help of four or five others, he raised the magnificent edifice you can see today. It contains some beautiful mosaics, and behind the altar is a modern chapel, with the most stunning glass window, which was created by the monks themselves.

⑤ Leave the Abbey complex via a stone gateway immediately opposite the one through which you entered, near the restaurant. This takes you into **Buckfast Road**. Follow it round to the left and at the junction go straight on into **Grange Road**. After about 1/4 mile you will leave the village and soon after that there is a junction; follow the main lane round to the right. At the next junction, a few yards further on, turn right (signposted to **Hembury Woods**). The lane climbs into the wood. After a little over 1/2 mile you will see a car park and picnic area on your left. Opposite it is a path; take it.

The path takes you deeper into the pretty wood. After a few yards look out for some steps and a path on the left; there is a post on the right with an arrow pointing to the fort. Turn up here and follow it as it winds and climbs steeply up through the trees. It crosses another path and continues to climb. Towards the top it joins another path; bear right. Soon you will cross a stile and then bend to the left to cross the outer ditch of the Iron Age hillfort of **Hembury Castle**. Follow the path through the fortifications.

The path leaves the fort through the northern rampart and you go through a gate. You emerge through another gate into a small car park; turn right in the lane beyond. At the first junction, 700 yards up the lane, go straight on. At the next, about the same distance further, turn left (signposted to **Holne**). You are now looking straight out over the area of moor you covered at the start of the walk, which should make you feel good and give you added energy for the last stretch! After another 1/2 mile you come to another junction; bear left (signposted to **Holne** and **Hexworthy**). About 1/4 mile further on, turn left (signposted to **Holne village centre** and **Buckfastleigh**). At the crossroads at the centre of the village you will find the **Church House Inn** on the other side if you are in need of refreshments. The car park is a few yards beyond it. (3 1/2 miles)

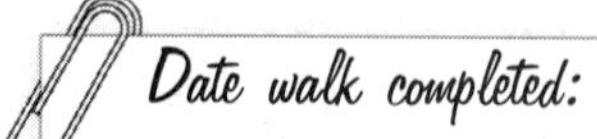

Walk 17

TWO CASTLES: COMPTON AND BERRY POMEROY VIA GREEN LANES

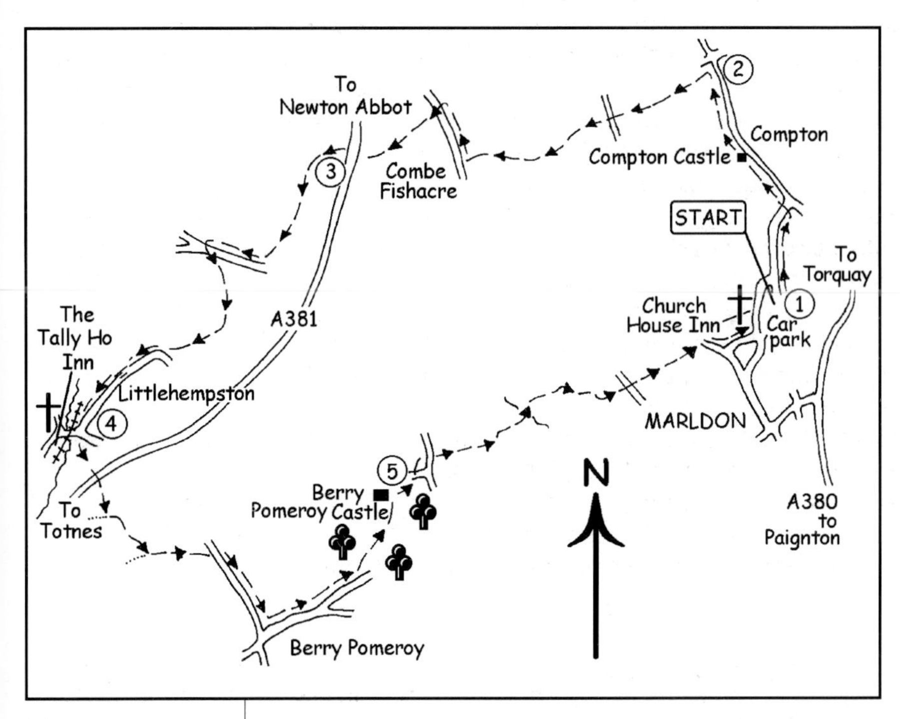

Distance:
$10\frac{1}{2}$ miles

Starting point:
The public car park in Marldon. GR 866636

Maps: OS Explorer 110 Torquay and Dawlish; OS Landranger 202 Torbay and South Dartmoor

How to get there: *Marldon is just west of the A380 Torbay Ring Road.Turn west off the A380 at the Preston Down junction and at the second roundabout turn right, following the sign for the Church House Inn. Follow this road for $\frac{1}{2}$ mile until you see the Church House Inn on your left. The car park is immediately opposite.*

Because they no longer carry traffic, green lanes provide a refuge for a wonderful variety of flora and fauna. And this delightful corner of South Devon is particularly well endowed with them. This lovely route follows a few of these ancient, half-forgotten byways, visiting two fascinating but very different historic castles and one particularly picturesque village along the way. An added bonus is the superb view you get across the undulating farmland to Dartmoor for much of the walk – and another is the fact that there are few hills to climb, and those that there are tend to be either very short or very gentle. Mud can be a problem in places, however, so appropriate footwear is recommended.

The Tally Ho Inn, at Littlehempston, is a lovely 14th-century inn that just oozes charm and character. Its granite walls, low ceilings and ancient beams give it a snug, cosy atmosphere, which is enhanced by the open fire at one end of the long bar and the wood-burning stove halfway along one wall. There is only the one bar, but outside there is a pretty garden.

Their food *is renowned locally, and includes both traditional favourites such as steaks and chicken and more adventurous dishes like ostrich and wild boar. Fresh local fish is also on offer – indeed, all their dishes are made from local ingredients wherever possible. For those with smaller appetites, there are sandwiches, salads and ploughman's lunches. Telephone: 01803 862316.*

The Walk

① Turn right as you leave the car park and follow the narrow lane out of the village and round to the right. At the T-junction turn left. The lane curves right past some pretty cottages and then left again. You pass **Compton** and then you will find **Compton Castle** on your left.

Compton Castle, a fortified manor, was built between the 14th and 16th centuries. It is now a National Trust property. The courtyard, great hall, solar, chapel, kitchen and rose garden are open to the public on certain days in summer (telephone 01803 875740 for details).

To continue the walk, carry on along the lane. After another 1/2 mile or so, you will come to a

BERRY POMEROY CASTLE

junction, with a lane going off to **North Whilborough** on the right. Turn left up a green lane (signposted as **Windthorn Lane**) – the first of many you will be following during the course of the walk. (1½ miles)

② The green lane climbs slightly, bordered by high hedges full of flowers and birds in summer. You get some attractive views over to the left as you climb. After levelling off for a bit it climbs again, but still gently, and narrows. You emerge at a lane; cross straight over into **Tanyard Lane**. Pause as you do so to look back over the undulating farmland.

Tanyard Lane continues to climb for a while. As it levels off, look to your right over the hedge and through gateways for a magnificent view across the farms and woods to **Dartmoor**, with the distinctive outline of **Haytor** silhouetted against the skyline. It is lovely and peaceful up here; the modern world seems a long way away and the silence is broken only by the breeze in the trees and the occasional bird. You cross another green lane; go straight on. After a while you begin to descend and a new vista of rolling farmland and hills opens up ahead to complement the moorland view on the right.

Three-quarters of a mile after joining **Tanyard Lane** you pass through a pretty copse and join a drive; follow it down to a lane and turn right. You pass through the hamlet of **Combe Fishacre**, with the imposing **Combe Fishacre House** on the right. You will come to the

Gate House on your right, followed by **Normans Farm**. Just opposite the latter turn left up another green lane (signposted as an unmetalled road). As you follow this you continue to get good views across to **Dartmoor** through the gateways on the right. After 1/2 mile you come out at the A381 **Newton Abbot to Totnes** road. (2 miles)

③ Turn right, and after about 30 yards turn left, just before a house called **Bow Grange**, up another green lane, this one surfaced. The moorland views are now ahead of you. After 250 yards the green lane goes to the left and you come to a junction; carry straight on. You pass a small copse and swing to the right past some farm buildings. You finally emerge onto a lane; turn right. After about 300 yards you will see a house called **Broadmead** on the right; just beyond it turn sharp left down another green lane (if you come to a road junction, you have gone too far and need to backtrack slightly).

As you follow this green lane the view across the farms to Dartmoor reappears. You will find yourself climbing quite steeply for a short while, and at the top of the hill your green lane crosses another; turn right here. You now get the best view yet. You emerge on a lane; bear right. As you do so you will

THE TALLY HO INN, LITTLEHEMPSTON

see the tower of the church at **Littlehempston** ahead of you, acting as a beacon to guide you to the delightful **Tally Ho Inn**, which is right next door. The lane goes steeply downhill to a T-junction. To visit the lovely little village of **Littlehempston** (and the **Tally Ho Inn**) turn right and follow the lane under the railway line, across the **River Hems** and round to the left. (2 miles)

④ After your rest at the **Tally Ho**, retrace your steps across the river and under the railway bridge and continue along the lane, past the junction where you came down. A hundred yards beyond it you will find a small lane going off to the right; follow it past a pretty thatched cottage and continue along the green lane beyond. It climbs briefly and after 300 yards you come to the main A381 road again. Cross straight over and follow another green lane up a hill. It is quite a stiff climb but not too long, and if you pause as you go you can look back and across to the moor again.

At the top is a T-junction; turn left and after a few yards, when you are faced by a gate, follow the green lane round to the right. You cross another green lane and continue to climb between high hedges, but a bit more gently now. You come to another T-junction; turn left. As you do so, a new vista opens up over the **South Hams hills** to the coast. You come to a lane; turn right. The view across the rich, undulating farmland is now ahead of you, with the tower of **Berry Pomeroy church** in the middle distance.

Follow the lane as it swings right to enter the village. At the roundabout turn left (signposted to the castle, **Marldon** and **Torquay**). You pass a school and leave the village. The road twists and winds up a hill; it is quite busy, so watch out for traffic. After just over 1/4 mile you will see a lane going off to the left (signposted to **Berry Pomeroy Castle** and **Afton**). Turn down it; as you go you will renew your acquaintance with the moorland view through gateways on the left. After another 1/4 mile or so you will come to the drive to the castle on your left. Turn down it and you will be met by a 180° panorama to the moors half-left. Follow the drive for 600 yards or so to the castle. (2 3/4 miles)

The ancient ruin of Berry Pomeroy Castle is said to be haunted by no fewer than four ghosts, all members of the Pomeroy family, who held the castle from soon after the Norman Conquest to the 16th century. The ruin is now in the hands of English Heritage (telephone 01803 866618 for opening times).

⑤ The large tree just to the right of

the castle, before you get to the car park, is called the **Wishing Tree**, and it is said that if you walk around it backwards three times your wish will come true. Immediately beyond it you will see a path going down the hill. Take that. It descends steeply at first, through the lovely wood, and then levels off. It comes out at a lane; bear right, and at the T-junction after a few yards turn left. As the lane curves left to cross a stream turn right up a surfaced green lane, following the public bridleway sign.

The green lane climbs for a while and then bends to the left. At the fork, where the surfaced lane goes on to **Loventor Manor**, bear right, following the direction of the public bridleway sign again. You pass some houses and the green lane narrows for a short while before broadening again. It crosses a stream and bends left. This is a rather muddy patch, but the lane soon becomes drier again. About 100 yards beyond the stream you will see a public footpath sign pointing right; follow it to a gate.

Keep to the right of the field on the other side and cross a stile at the end. Follow the fence round to the right and at the end follow it round to the left – do not go through the gate. As you go you can enjoy the moorland view again on your left, with **Haytor** making another appearance on the horizon. Cross another stile and keep to the right of the next field. At the end go round to the left again. Go up some steps and across a stile at the end, into a lane.

Turn right and then almost immediately left up a drive. After a few yards turn right through a gate and climb some steep steps through trees. At the top go through a kissing gate and keep to the right of the hedge on the other side. At the end of the field cross a stone stile and follow the path on the other side as it winds between a hedge and a fence. You emerge through a kissing gate onto a playing field; keep to the left and cross a stile at the end. Follow the short path on the other side to a lane; turn right. After 150 yards you will see **Church Hill** going off to the left; go down it. It leads steeply down to the church; you can either follow it all the way to the bottom and turn left or turn off through the attractive churchyard and come out in front of the **Church House Inn**. (2¼ miles)

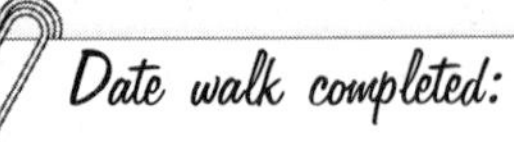

INDUSTRIAL REMAINS IN A WOODLAND SETTING: THE PLYM VALLEY

CANN VIADUCT

Distance:
8½ miles

Starting point:
The car park on the eastern side of Plym Bridge. GR 524586

Maps: OS Explorer OL20 South Devon; OS Landranger 201 Plymouth and Launceston

How to get there: *Plym Bridge is 1½ miles north of Plympton, on the outskirts of Plymouth. Turn north off the main road through Plympton between the A38 and Plymouth, following the signs to Plym Bridge. Alternatively you can approach from the A386 Plymouth to Tavistock road. Turn east just north of the airport to Estover and follow the signs from there. There are car parks on both sides of the river, but cars cannot cross Plym Bridge itself.*

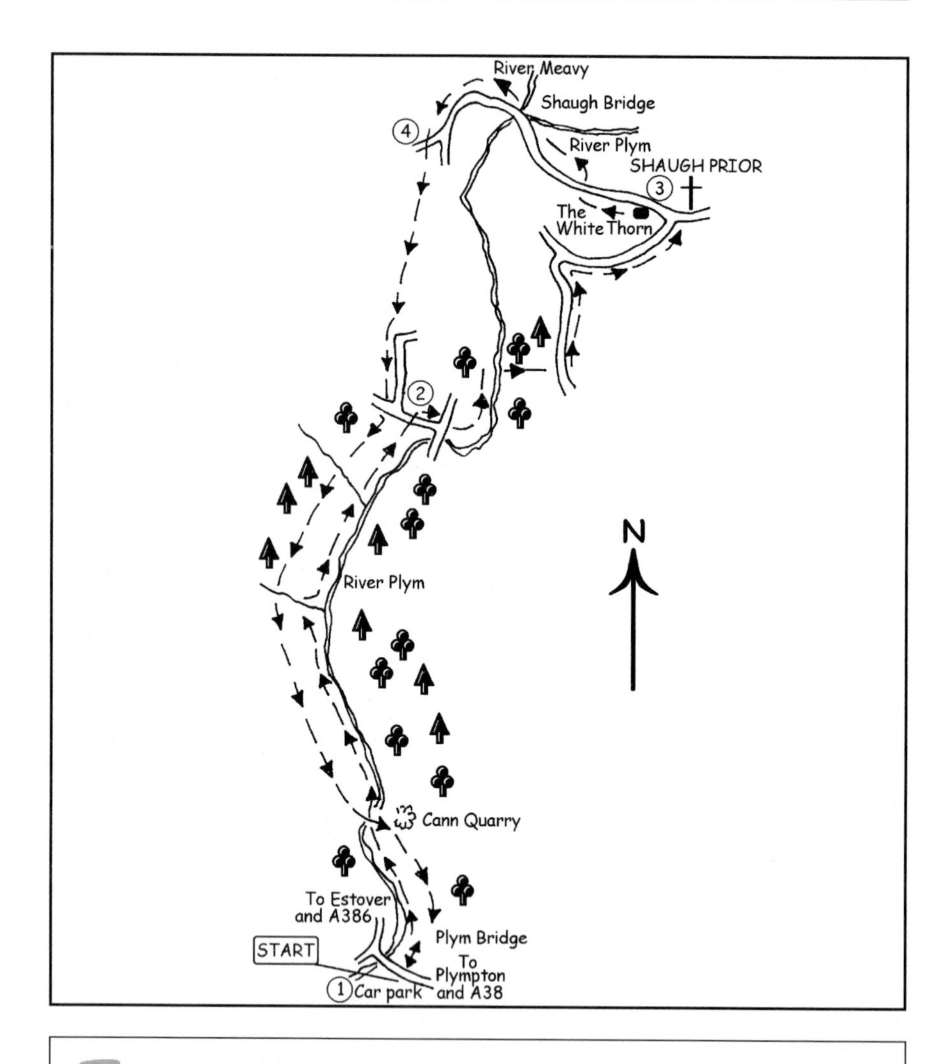

This is a walk for those who like woods and water. It follows the lovely, heavily wooded Bickleigh Vale upstream along the bank of the River Plym, and returns along the spectacular bed of the old South Devon and Tavistock Railway high above the valley. Along the way there are a number of sites of industrial archaeological interest to see, as well as wildlife galore. Moreover, apart from some fairly stiff climbing in the middle of the route, it is all remarkably easy going.

Despite its appearance, the White Thorn was built as recently as 1936. The original White Thorn was next door (the building is now two cottages, appropriately enough called White Thorn Cottage and Old White Thorn Cottage). But its beamed ceiling, horse brasses and fireplace give it the atmosphere of an older establishment. It comprises one long room, with a pool table and armchairs at one end, the bar area in the middle and a dining area beyond. There is also an attractive beer garden with a superb children's play area.

It has developed *a reputation for its food – all home cooked, using local produce where possible. There are snacks such as toasted sandwiches and baguettes and main meals which range from steaks and local sausages to fish and vegetarian dishes. Telephone: 01752 839245.*

The Walk

① Cross the lane from the car park and go through a gate onto the towpath of an old canal. You pass under a railway bridge and then you will find the mainly dry canal bed on your right and the swiftly flowing river on your left. This is the National Trust's **Plymbridge Woods**, and you will find yourself surrounded by trees, mainly beech.

These delightful woods, which stretch for over 5 miles up the Plym Valley, are a haven for wildlife of all sorts. Among the animals you may see, apart from the ubiquitous squirrels, are foxes and fallow deer. There are dippers, kingfishers and herons on the water and buzzards, peregrines and a host of woodland birds in the surrounding area.

After a while you lose the river briefly but keep the canal bed on your right. Then the canal gives way to a large pipeline. A little under 3/4 mile after starting out the path and the river curve to the right and go under **Cann Viaduct**. On the other side you can see the remains of **Cann Quarry**.

The impressive Cann slate quarry dates from the 17th century, and supplied slate for a number of buildings, including Devonport Dockyard.

Cann Viaduct was built in 1905 to replace a wooden structure built by Isambard Kingdom Brunel in 1859 to carry the South Devon and Tavistock Railway over the River Plym. The railway was closed in 1962.

Turn right and climb some steps to the viaduct; at the top you will see the **Railway Cottages** on your left. Turn right again to cross the viaduct. On the other side you will see a path going off to the left, with a post on the right marked with blue and red stripes. Go down the path and on your right you will see the remains of the **Rumple Quarry**.

Carry on round to the left and at the bottom turn sharp left to continue upstream along the river bank. It is quite delightful along here, with the river running noisily down on your right, the woods stretching up the steep hill on your left and glimpses of the occasional spectacular railway viaduct. You cross a few footbridges and will see paths and steps leading off to the left; ignore these and continue alongside the river. You will pass one field and then cross a stile into another, but this is just a small clearing in the surrounding woodland.

About $^1/_2$ mile after crossing **Cann Viaduct**, you pass under another viaduct and turn right to cross a footbridge over a tributary of the **Plym**, then right again to rejoin the main river. You enter a conifer plantation and pass a flow-measuring station. About $^3/_4$ mile after crossing the stream you come to a fork; turn left to climb up the side of the valley (if you miss the turning, it doesn't matter as you will

THE WHITE THORN, SHAUGH PRIOR

soon come to a large gate barring your way). It is a steep climb, and at the top you emerge onto a lane; turn right. (2¼ miles)

② It seems unfair, but having climbed all the way out of the valley you now have to go back down into it. It is a steep descent, and at the bottom is a T-junction. Immediately opposite is a gate with a stile alongside; cross the stile and follow the path on the other side straight down among some trees. When you get to the bottom of the hill, follow the path round to the left through a wood, alongside the river once again. After a while you cross another stile (which was broken when I last walked this route). Keep to the right of the field on the other side and re-enter the wood. You soon come to a junction in the path; turn right to cross a stile, a footbridge and another stile. Continue through the trees on the other side to a field; keep to the right and at the end cross a stile into a conifer plantation.

Climb through the trees to a track; cross it and continue climbing through the plantation on the other side. You emerge via a stile onto a lane; turn left. The lane winds downhill and then uphill again. After ½ mile you come to a T-junction; turn right. This lane climbs again, but you can encourage yourself with the thought that there is a pub at the top – and that apart from one very short and easy ascent it is pretty much downhill all the way from then on. When you get to the top of the hill, **Shaugh Prior** comes into view on the left, with the tower of the church dominating the village. The lane curves to the right and to the left and there is one last climb. At the T-junction at the top turn left to the **White Thorn** or right if you want to see the **Shaugh Prior cross and church**. (1¾ miles)

Set into a wall at a junction just east of the church, the ancient Shaugh Prior cross may have been a preaching cross, from which itinerant preachers would hold forth before the church was built.

③ Carry on along the lane through the village. Just beyond the derestriction sign you will see a surfaced track leading off to the right (there is a public footpath sign pointing to **Cadover**, but you cannot see it from the road). Turn off here and follow the track for a short distance. As it bends to the right you will see a dilapidated path sign on the left. Cross a stile into some open ground and follow the path on the other side into a wood. It goes down through the trees to another stile. Continue on the other side to a lane; turn right and after a few yards you will come to **Shaugh Bridge**. If you are looking for somewhere to have a picnic turn right and cross a footbridge beyond the car park on the right into the idyllic **Dewerstone Wood**.

Behind the car park are the ruins of some 19th-century china clay works.

Cross **Shaugh Bridge** and follow the lane round to the right and then to the left. At the junction go straight on (signposted to **Bickleigh** and **Roborough**). The lane winds and climbs slightly, and after another 500 yards you come to another junction. Turn right and follow a small lane for about 100 yards until you see a gate on your right; go through it and you will find yourself once again on the bed of the old **South Devon and Tavistock Railway**. (1¼ miles)

④ Turn left and follow the line under a bridge. It runs through a lovely deciduous wood, which slopes steeply down to the river on the left. After about ½ mile you cross a viaduct, high above the valley, and 300 yards beyond that you emerge onto a lane. Turn right and follow the lane round to the left. After ¼ mile you come to a T-junction; turn left (signposted for the **Plym Valley** cycle path to **Plympton**). Two hundred yards down this lane turn right, back onto the railway track, following the sign for the **Plym Valley Path** once again.

After ¼ mile you cross another viaduct. Pause as you do so to enjoy the view across the treetops, especially on your left, and if you have the head for it, look down to see the river over 100 feet below you, with the path you followed on the outward leg alongside it. You cross another, equally spectacular viaduct almost ¾ mile further on, and pass under two bridges.

Another ½ mile or so brings you to **Cann Viaduct** again. Cross it, but instead of turning off onto the riverside path, carry on along the railway bed. You will pass the **Railway Cottages** on your left. You go under a bridge and should be able to see the canal bed down below you on the left. Half a mile after leaving **Cann Viaduct** you cross a bridge over a lane; turn left on the other side to return to the car park. (3¼ miles)

THE PRIMROSE LINE: LODDISWELL AND THE AVON VALLEY

THE OLD LODDISWELL STATION, NOW A PRIVATE HOUSE

Distance:
9 miles

Starting point:
The public car park at Blackdown Rings, GR 718519; or the public car park in Loddiswell if you are starting there. GR 719485

Maps: OS Explorer OL20 South Devon; OS Landranger 202 Torquay and South Dartmoor

How to get there: *Take the A3121 south from the A38 and follow the signs for Loddiswell, or turn north off the A381 just outside Kingsbridge, following the signs for Loddiswell again. Blackdown Rings is to the east of this road about 2½ miles north of Loddiswell and is clearly signposted. (If you are approaching from the Kingsbridge area you may prefer to start the walk at Loddiswell – point 3 in the route description.)*

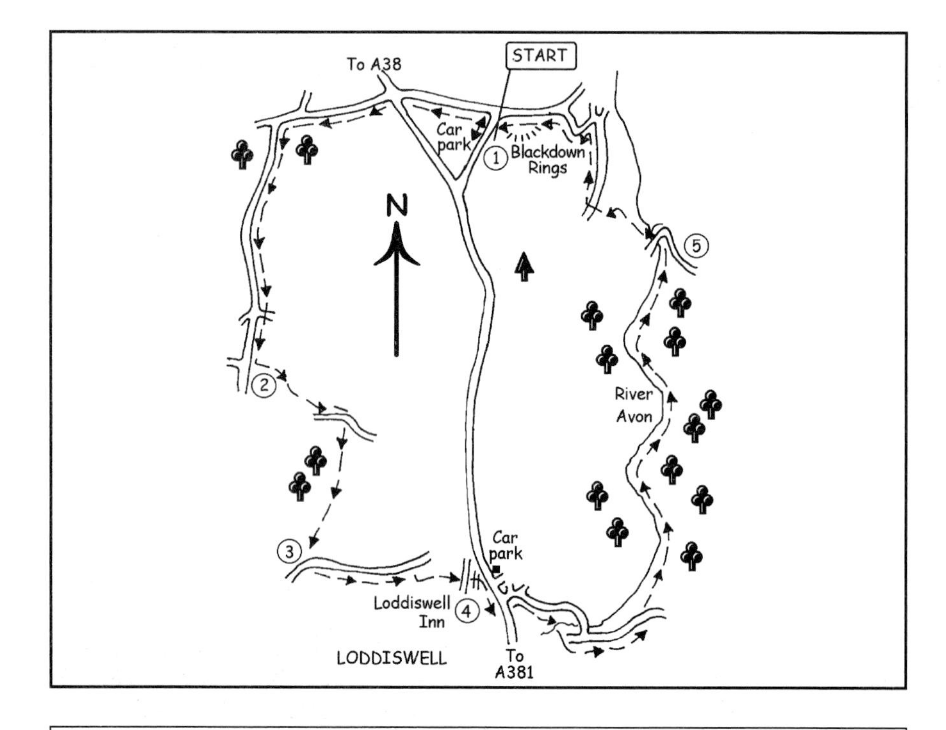

This is a delightful walk, full of interest. After exploring the Iron Age and Norman fortifications of the Blackdown Rings – and taking in the superb views to be enjoyed from them – you follow flower-filled lanes and tracks south to the pretty village of Loddiswell. The return route follows a disused railway up the beautiful valley of the River Avon through a series of woods. There is a stiff climb out of the valley at the end, but otherwise it is very easy walking.

The Blackdown Rings have been used several times for the defence of the local area. It was originally an Iron Age hillfort, with a massive rampart and a deep ditch – both of which are still clearly visible – enclosing an area of about 5 acres. Situated on the crest of the Blackdown Ridge, it is in an excellent defensive position, an advantage that recommended it to the Normans a millennium or so later. They built a motte and bailey castle in the north-west corner of the site in the 11th or 12th century, and the remains of that can also still be seen today.

The Loddiswell Inn, halfway round the route, is a 200-year-old coaching inn with an interesting history. It served as a holding jail where prisoners were held pending transfer to a proper prison – not as pleasant a prospect as it may sound, as they were securely locked up, well away from the temptations of the flesh! It is a delightful pub, full of character, with low beams and a mixture of stone, brick and panelled walls.

The bar has interesting little nooks, which gives it a warm, cosy feeling. Up some steps at the end is a very pleasant eating area and outside you will find a terrace overlooking the centre of the village, where you can sit and 'people watch'. Both locals and visitors are given a warm welcome.

The food *ranges from sandwiches to a variety of daily specials, including fresh fish, as well as vegetarian and meat dishes. The Sunday roasts are particularly renowned. Telephone: 01548 550308.*

① You will begin to appreciate the view almost before you have got out of your car – rolling farmland stretching away to the south towards the sea. When you have explored the **Blackdown Rings**, leave via the car park, turning right into the lane. At the T-junction at the end, turn left. Almost immediately you get another lovely view over to your right, all the way to Dartmoor. At the junction at the main road, go straight across. At the next junction, about $1/2$ mile further on, bear left. You continue to enjoy the view across to Dartmoor on your right.

After another 150 yards turn left (signposted to **Chillaton**, **Lixton** and **Aveton Gifford**). This is a lovely woodland stretch, and from time to time you get another good view through gateways on the left. The lane is fringed with flowers throughout the summer, and as you come over the brow of the hill, yet another beautiful vista opens up ahead of you. After 1 mile you come to a crossroads; go straight on (signposted to **Lixton**, **Aveton Gifford** and **Kingsbridge**). ($2^1/2$ miles)

② At the next junction go straight on again (signposted to **Aveton Gifford** and **Kingsbridge**) and a few yards beyond it you will see a track leading off to the left, signposted as a public byway to **Beer Hill**. Turn into it and when you come to a gate into a field about 500 yards along turn right down a green lane. This is a lovely, quiet stretch; as you descend between high banks topped by trees you get occasional glimpses into the valley on your right.

After another 500 yards you emerge onto a surfaced lane; bear left. Then 150 yards further on, just before the lane crosses a bridge, you will come to a public bridleway sign on the right. Turn off here and cross a field to a gap in a line of trees on the other side. Cross the next field, aiming for the wood you can see half-left. You go round the bottom of a small hill to a gate hidden behind some bushes at the end.

Follow the path on the other side to another gate, which leads into a wood. The path goes through the wood for a while to another gate; beyond that it runs along the edge of the trees, with a stream a little distance away on the left. You go through one more gate and head up to a drive. When you reach it, bear right, following the direction of the waymark arrow. This path takes you round a small field to a lane; turn left. (1¼ miles)

③ Follow the lane past a farmhouse and down a hill. After about 700 yards you pass **Higher Yanston Farm** on the left, and about 200 yards beyond it you will see a public footpath sign pointing

THE LODDISWELL INN

through the hedge on the right. Follow its direction and climb some steps into a field and cross to a gate in the far left-hand corner. Keep to the right of the next field to another gate, and keep to the right again. At the end of the next field cross a stile into a lane. You are now on the outskirts of **Loddiswell**.

This is a fascinating village, with a network of little lanes around the centre just asking to be explored. It is somewhat unusual in that the pretty 14th-century church is on the edge of the village rather than being its focal point. If it has a centre, it could be said to be the village pub.

Congratulations – you are now halfway through your walk, and probably feel you could do with a celebratory drink. To get it, cross the lane to a stone stile leading to a path between hedges. This path emerges at a road; cross it and take the surfaced path on the other side, alongside some modern houses. It comes out at the main road through the village; turn right and you will find the **Loddiswell Inn** on your left. (1 mile)

④ Turn left at the pub and almost immediately fork right down **Well Street**; at the next junction, follow the main lane round to the right. It takes you out of the village and down steeply into the valley of the River Avon. You pass the **Avon Mill Garden Centre** and cross the river. At the T-junction on the other side, turn left. The lane swings right under a bridge; at the junction just beyond, follow the main lane round to the left. When you come to the old **Loddiswell Station** and the lane curves right, go straight on and cross a stile to the right of the house onto a path into a wood. After a short distance you will see a stile on the left; cross it and turn right to follow the track of the dismantled **Kingsbridge and Salcombe Railway**.

This 12½ mile branch line was started in the 1860s, to run from the main line at South Brent to Kingsbridge, but was abandoned before it was completed. It was taken over by the Great Western Railway and opened in 1893. The passenger service never really took off, however, and by the 1930s it was used mainly by summer visitors enthralled by the beautiful route. It still carried a great deal of freight, however, and was not completely closed until 1963. Because of its lovely setting, particularly this stretch along the banks of the Avon, it is called the Primrose Line locally.

The track runs for ¾ mile through the lovely wood, with the river rippling over the rocks on the left and birds calling in the trees and swooping over the water. If you are planning a picnic there are several places to stop along the bank. It finally crosses over the river; when it does so, bear right along a path that continues along the bank. After another 1/2 mile of beautiful woodland walking you cross a stone stile and then a wooden stile on the left, and climb back up to the disused railway track. Bear right.

About 500 yards after rejoining the railway track you climb up away from the river. After a short distance you will find a bit of wooden fence on your left; go through a gap in it and down some steps back to the river. Cross a small footbridge and continue alongside the river for a while until the path turns right and emerges via a stile onto a lane. (2 1/2 miles)

⑤ Turn left and pass some pretty cottages to a junction; go left to cross **Topsham Bridge**. On the other side turn right, following the public footpath sign. Climb to cross the railway track again and go through a kissing gate into another wood. Cross a little stream and then a stile into a field; keep to the right and then go up to a gate in the fence ahead.

Turn left immediately beyond the gate and climb steeply up the side of a field; at the top follow the hedge to the right. At the end cross a stile into a lane; turn right. Pass a farm and at the fork, go straight on, passing the sign for **Hazelwood House**. After 250 yards you pass an old chapel on the right; at the fork beyond it go left and then a few yards further on turn very sharp left. The lane begins to climb steeply, but there is a good view over to the left as you go. The lane swings to the right, still climbing; pause from time to time to admire the outlook to the right over the Avon valley. You eventually come to a junction with another lane; turn left and after 500 yards of more gentle climbing turn left again to return to the **Blackdown Rings** car park. (1 3/4 mile)

Walk 20

LITERARY MEMORIES: BIGBURY BAY

THE RUINS OF A LIME KILN ON WONWELL BEACH

Distance:
9 miles

Starting point:
The beach car park at Bigbury-on-Sea. GR 651441

Maps: OS Explorer OL20 South Devon; OS Landranger 202 Torbay and South Dartmoor

How to get there: *Bigbury-on-Sea is at the end of the B3392, which runs south from the A379 between Aveton Gifford and Modbury. There is a large public car park by the beach. If that is full, there is another one at the top of the village, on the way in.*

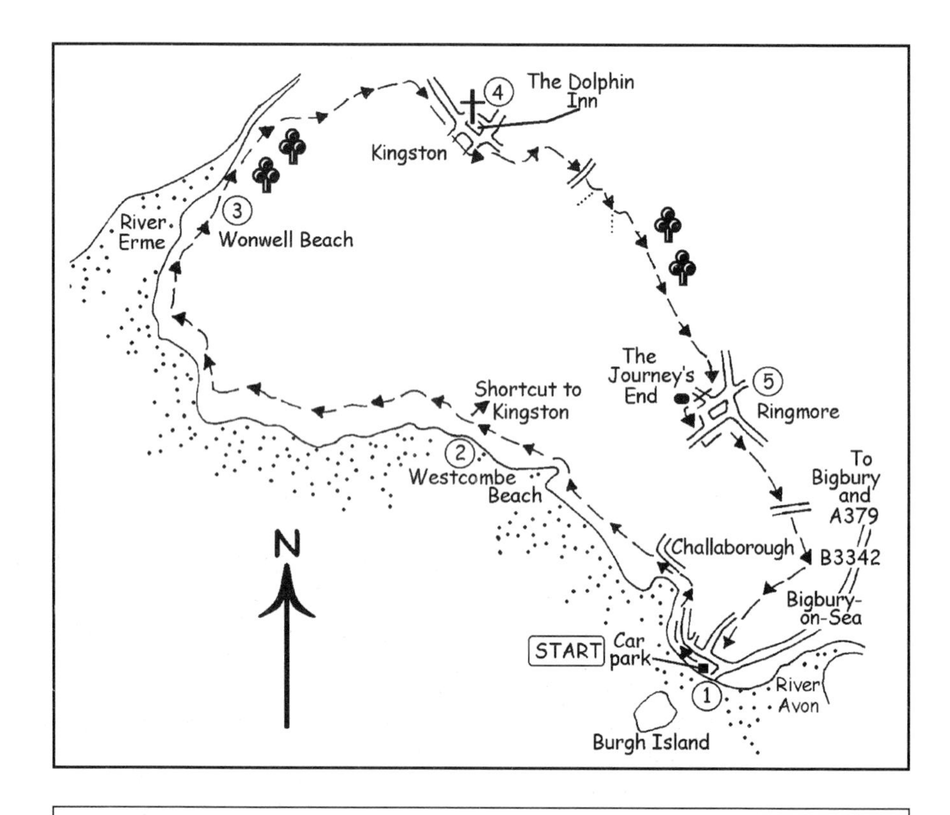

This is a magnificent outing, taking you around the stunningly beautiful Bigbury Bay, with outstanding views along the coast in both directions. The return leg is just as lovely, following farm paths across the rolling South Hams hills (with more superb views) and visiting two delightful little villages along the way. It is not a walk for the unfit or faint-hearted, however: there is a price to pay for the views, in the form of several steep hills, especially along the Coast Path.

Originally called St Michael's, Burgh Island, which is just off the coast by the car park, has literary connections. Its hotel was built in 1929, and had Noel Coward as one of its guests. Agatha Christie, who lived not far away and also spent time here, used it as the setting for two of her novels, *And Then There Were None* and *Evil Under the Sun*.

The lovely 16th-century Dolphin Inn sits in the middle of Kingston, beside the church. It has thick stone walls, shuttered windows and low beamed ceilings, and oozes atmosphere. As the landlord says, it hasn't changed over the years – even the regulars are the same! There are three main areas, one of which is non-smoking, and they are all decorated in the same style, with a wide variety of mugs and a collection of foreign bank notes pinned to the beams. Across the lane is a large garden with swings for children.

The food *is all good, home-cooked fare, and ranges from bar snacks to main meals and daily specials. The chef's speciality is fish, although he does a very good job of meat and vegetarian dishes as well! Telephone: 01548 810314.*

The Walk

① Turn left as you leave the car park and follow a surfaced lane, following the **Coast Path** sign. You will immediately be met by a lovely view ahead along the coast. Cross a road to another car park and continue along a road on the other side into the village. The road ends and you follow a track to a gate. Go past it and follow a path down a hill towards **Challaborough**. At the bottom you join a road; follow it round the beach and when it swings sharp right look to your left and you will see a Coast Path sign pointing up the cliff to the right; follow it. It is a bit of a climb, but at the top the path runs along the edge of the cliff and you get another good view ahead and also back, past **Burgh Island**.

You pass a path going right to **Ringmore** and then descend steeply to **Aymer Cove**. At the bottom you pass another path to Ringmore, cross a footbridge and then see a third path to Ringmore. I am afraid that our route follows none of them, but instead climbs the hill up ahead. It is a fairly short climb and then the path levels off. At the top you come to yet another path to Ringmore on the right; ignore that as well, and continue to enjoy the views as you follow the Coast Path. Soon you will see **Westcombe Beach** ahead of you, with a steep descent to it. Of, course, a steep descent usually means a steep ascent on the other side, and this is no exception to the rule. The climb up on the other side of the beach is a particularly stiff one, but if you think it looks too daunting you can take a short cut from here and rejoin the walk at **Kingston**; just turn right on the other side of the stream which runs across the beach and follow the path to Kingston. (1¾ miles)

② The Coast Path goes through a gate beyond the stream and climbs steeply, zigzagging up the hill. As you can see, it is a stiff climb, but if you take it gently (and perhaps stop to catch your breath at the strategically placed seat halfway up) you will enjoy the outlook when you reach the top. There is now a new view to the right across the lovely **South Hams** countryside.

You go down a bit, but more gently. Go through a gate and follow the yellow waymarked stakes across a field. Go through another gate and then through another. The path takes you round to the left and then to the right round a headland, and the **Erme estuary** comes into view. When you round the next headland keep to the bottom of the field to reach a stile. The path then takes you down to cross another stile to **Wonwell Beach**. (2¼ miles)

THE DOLPHIN INN, KINGSTON

③ Cross a small stream and just on the other side you will see a path going right away from the beach. Take that and follow it round to the left behind the beach. It then runs up alongside the estuary and enters some trees. As it does so, look out on your left for the first of the ruined kilns of the **Wonwell** lime works. Soon after you will see **Wonwell Slip**. This slipway was used until 1917 to import coal and limestone for the works. Beyond it, right on the beach, is another ruined kiln. The path emerges onto a lane just above the slipway.

Turn right and follow the lane for 150 yards until you come to a public footpath sign pointing right, indicating the way to **Kingston**. Turn off here and follow the path as it climbs through a lovely wood. It winds through the trees and then goes along the edge of the wood until it eventually emerges via a stile into a field. Keep to the right; as you go you get a superb view on the left across the fields and woods to **Dartmoor**. Cross another stile and keep to the right of the next field. A third stile takes you onto a short path between hedges, and a fourth takes you into yet another field; keep to the right again. There is a fifth stile; in the field beyond go straight across, following the public footpath sign.

When you come to the far boundary, turn left and follow it, crossing another stile. Keep to the right of the next field and cross the last stile into a lane. Turn right and follow the lane down to **Kingston**. At the T-junction turn left and pass the pretty church. Immediately beyond it turn right and you will see the **Dolphin Inn** on your right; after all your climbing it is probably an extremely welcome sight! (1½ miles)

④ When you leave the pub turn right, away from the church, and at the T-junction turn right again. Take the next turning on the left and follow the lane out of the village. When the lane ends, turn left, following the sign for **Ringmore**. Cross a stone stile and turn right along a clear path through some trees, with a series of ornamental ponds on your right. At the end, cross a stile on the left and keep to the left of the field on the other side.

At the end of the field turn right and continue alongside the hedge to a stile. Keep to the left of the next field to another stile, which leads into a lane. Turn left and after a few yards right again, following the sign to **Ringmore**. Go straight across the next field, with a lovely view across to the coast ahead of you. Cross another stile to a track; turn left and then right along the track. After about 200 yards, look out for a yellow-waymarked post pointing through a gateway on the left. Go through and follow the track along the edge of a field. At the end turn right to skirt the field. About 150 yards along this edge the path goes left and downhill through an attractive wood.

At the bottom it swings right to follow the valley of a stream you can hear on your left (although you can't see it through the undergrowth). Cross a stile and continue along the valley across some open ground. You eventually cross a stream by the ruins of **Noddon Mill**. Climb the path up the hill on the other side. Cross a stile on your right and climb up a field to another stile. Turn left and in the far corner of the field go right through a kissing gate. Keep to the left of the next field and after a short distance go through another kissing gate on the left. Go straight across the next field to a gate with a kissing gate alongside it. Bear left beyond it to yet another kissing gate, which leads you into a lane; turn right. Pass the church and at the T-junction turn right to **Ringmore**. (2 miles)

⑤ To carry straight on with the walk, follow the main lane round to the left (signposted to **Challaborough**), and when it bends right go straight on along a side lane. If you want to explore **Ringmore** a little, and perhaps visit a pub, turn right down the hill, and then left at the junction lower down. The **Journey's End** in the village can be thoroughly recommended (telephone: 01548 810205).

The writer R.C. Sherriff is said to have written part of his anti-war play* Journey's End *while staying at what was then the New Inn, Ringmore, soon after the First World War, which prompted the landlord to change its name.

To continue the walk from the pub, take the lane that runs up the hill to the left just beyond it. At the T-junction turn left, and when the lane bends left turn right along a side lane; this is where you rejoin the route that by-passed the centre of the village. Follow the lane past some houses and out of the village. At the end, go through a kissing gate and straight on along the right-hand edge of the field. At the bottom go through a gap in the fence and then go right through a gap in the bank on the right. On the other side turn left through a kissing gate and go down the hill between the bank and hedge on your left and a fence on your right.

Go through a gate at the bottom and then cross a stile and a stone footbridge. Climb up the left-hand side of the next field, and at the top go through a gate on the left into a lane. Turn right and immediately left across a stile, following the footpath sign. Go straight across a field, down the hill to a track; cross it and go through a kissing gate. I am afraid that you have to climb the hill beyond, but it is not a very long climb. At the top cross a stile and then climb a little bit more to a gate. Keep to the left and in the corner of the field, turn right to follow a track.

Cross a stile and keep to the left of the next field. As you go you can see **Burgh Island** ahead of you. Go through a gap in the wall and continue along the left-hand side of the next field. At the end cross a stile into a road on the edge of **Bigbury-on-Sea**. Follow the road down to the car park. (1½ miles)

Date walk completed: